HAGEN-RENAKER POTTERY
Horses & Other Figurines

Nancy Kelly

Schiffer ® *Publishing Ltd*
4880 Lower Valley Road, Atglen, PA 19310 USA

Designed by Bonnie M. Hensley
Typeset in Zurich Blk BT/Souvenir Lt BT

ISBN: 0-7643-1039-9
Printed in China
1 2 3 4

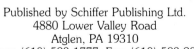

Published by Schiffer Publishing Ltd.
4880 Lower Valley Road
Atglen, PA 19310
Phone: (610) 593-1777; Fax: (610) 593-2002
E-mail: Schifferbk@aol.com
Please visit our web site catalog at **www.schifferbooks.com**

In Europe, Schiffer books are distributed by Bushwood Books
6 Marksbury Avenue Kew Gardens
Surrey TW9 4JF England
Phone: 44 (0)208-392-8585; Fax: 44 (0)208-392-9876
E-mail: Bushwd@aol.com

This book may be purchased from the publisher.
Include $3.95 for shipping. Please try your bookstore first.
We are interested in hearing from authors with book ideas on related subjects.
You may write for a free printed catalog.

Contents

Dedication & Acknowledgments

The story of the Hagen-Renaker pottery company involves many people, and is a fascinating story of grit, imagination, and courage. Some of the key contributors to this history are the members of the Renaker family, John and Maxine who started the company and gave the company life. Their children Jim, Susan, and Mary were also involved in the business and their memories help bring this story to life.

Other vital people include the designers whose talent and perseverance gave the company its character; Helen Perrin Farnlund, Maureen Love, Will Climes, Tom Masterson, Nell Bortells, Martha Hand, Robyn Sikking, Laurilyn Burson, Don Winton, and others. Their recollections and the artwork that they created and shared here help to develop the character of this story.

Finally, the dedicated staff who helped make the vision a reality also helped make this book a reality, too. Most notably, Bill Nicely, who worked at Hagen-Renaker from the early days to the present, provides much valuable background and insight as only an insider can. Pat O' Brien Kristof, former supervisor, and Claire Weller, former bookkeeper, also contribute to this story.

In addition I would like to thank the many people who helped by providing items for me to photograph, photos that they took, or information that they shared. These include Gayle Roller, Nancy Falzone, Tracy Phillips, William Wiemhoff, Ardith Carlton, Maggie Kennedy, Lisa Camerer, Dawn Sinkovich, Joan Berkwitz, Sue P. Stewart, Jane Chapman, Nancy Banks, Linda Walter, Bonnie Elber, Jenny Palmer, Teresa Rogers, Nancy Atkinson Young, Carolyn Boydston, Jayne Kubas, Linda Roberts, Joyce Streffon, Fran and Bob Wooster, Denny and Betty Hannigan, June Carson, Eric and Lina McDonald, and Ellen Adler. Special thanks to Richard C. Best for the use of his photographic equipment, and to Janet DeClark, Chadd Smith, Brad Angus, and Vern Scheck for taking such special care of my photos. Finally, thanks to my helpmate, friend, and husband John Kelly for assisting in so many ways, and for putting up with my hobby.

Note on Price Guide

This price guide is based on conservative estimates and actual observations of selling prices for unbroken figurines with good detail and color. Exceptional pieces could be worth more. The value of a piece is ultimately set by the buyer and seller, but this book should serve as a reasonable guide.

As one reads through this book, a variety of sticker styles will be noted. An attempt was made to show several types, and the age of the piece can sometimes be determined by the sticker. The older Designers' Workshop animals often wore name stickers, although sometimes they were switched in the case of two similar animals (for example, the Chihuahuas Carmencita and Pancho Villa). The Hagen-Renaker lines were also not clearly defined by size, but more by association. The Designers' Workshop pieces were approximately 2.5" and up, although some of the lying baby animals would be smaller than that. Likewise, the miniature line is approximately 2.5" and below, although some pieces are taller than that, depending on position.

Top right: This adorable little fellow arrived at my house recently; a totally unexpected, one-of-a-kind surprise from the wonderful folks at Hagen-Renaker!

Introduction:
In The Beginning

Excerpt from *One Lucky Kid*, by Maxine Hagen Renaker, 1992

Dad did so many *great deeds* to help me and my husband and our children that I can never feel I expressed *enough* gratitude when he was alive. For one thing, he gambled on John and me when we wanted to start our pottery business. Right after World War II, John and I decided that we would have a business of our own. John was pleased with some crude little figures I had made with some modeling clay, and he encouraged me to make models of little birds and animals. John had built our first kiln which we set up in our garage. This kiln was fired with gas brought to it from the kitchen by way of a garden hose.

Dad knew we were in earnest about this project and that we would certainly need a place to go forward and expand the efforts, so he decided, quite on his own, that he would furnish us with that necessary place. It was decided that we would settle in Monrovia where Mama, Dad and I had formerly lived from 1926 to 1929 and where John had been born and raised.

Dad was a very good carpenter, and he had earned enough money with his skill to buy an industrial lot in Monrovia. He then borrowed money on that lot to finance the needed building materials, which, incidentally, were in very short supply right after the war. He had friends in Oregon who were in the lumber business so he drove up to Medford and negotiated with his friends to supply him with a carload of lumber. That carload carried about three times as much lumber as he needed for the building for us, and he was able to sell the surplus to a local lumberyard. That money helped with the other building expenses.

Dad did all the carpentry by himself, but when it came to plumbing and electricity, his younger brother, my Uncle Arnie (who worked for the Bureau of Power and Light in Pomona) helped him with those complicated appliances. During that time both the brothers were working seven days a week. Uncle Arnie drove to Monrovia from Pomona on Saturdays and Sundays, his days off from his regular job, to help his brother, until the wiring and plumbing were finished.

When we moved from Culver City to Monrovia, it was quite impossible to find a house or apartment to rent, so Dad had also added just enough rooms onto the pottery building to house all of us temporarily. We moved into our new pottery-plus-apartment on Easter Sunday in 1946.

It was John who decided to name our company *Hagen*-Renaker Pottery to honor my father and Uncle Arnie, who had both made the progress of our efforts possible. As I write this, the pottery, which they helped us start and which has their name coupled with our name as its corporate title, is still going strong under the careful management of our daughter Susan.

John Renaker, October 1998

"Our workplace was the equivalent of two two-car garages side-by-side with room on the long side and on one of the short sides if you can visualize that. Maxine and I and three kids lived in three of the rooms. Her parents lived in one. There were no houses available right after the war. We had casting tables and kilns outside. We managed like that for six months. Not premises for gracious living or efficient working. To make up for it, post-war demand for anything in giftwares was powerful. We found other places to rent for production, and in three years were using eleven buildings of various sizes and adaptability and were living in a real house. A person has the strength or desperation to do things like that about once in a lifetime."

Jim Renaker, May 1998

"Do you know why the name was chosen? The family business in Monrovia was for many years the Renaker Company Morticians, a mortuary. My dad decided on that hyphenated name for his company because he certainly didn't want anybody to ring him up in the middle of the night to bury the dead!"

1

The Early Years

The Hagen-Renaker Pottery company is known for creating animal figurines of clay in Monrovia, California in the years following World War II. However, the story began before that. In 1944, while living in Culver City, California, John Renaker built his first kiln in his garage and began to learn about making pottery. His mother, Moss Renaker, had recommended that he look into making pottery for a living, since she worked as an artist for Joe Walker at Walker Pottery and recognized it as a booming business. Jim Renaker describes the fledgling Culver City business this way. "There they made jobber pieces. Jobbers were people who went around and farmed the farmer, so to speak. They had molds and could supply these molds to anyone who wanted to cast them, and they would take the ware back, and pay a certain amount of money for it. Not too many people did job-shop work, because following the war most of them went into business for themselves."

In 1945, John went to work for Walker Pottery and was able to learn the trade on a larger scale. During the year that he worked there, he mixed the slip (clay), handled the equipment, and developed the skills needed to start his own business. Meanwhile, Ole Hagen (Maxine's father), who was a carpenter by trade, purchased property on West Chestnut Street in Monrovia, California, and built the building that would be the birth place of the Hagen-Renaker Pottery company; a company which was the dream of his daughter and a company that bears his name first, along with the Renaker's family name. On the day after Easter in 1946, the Renakers moved into their new home, and John left Walker Pottery to work full time for the new company.

Helen Perrin (now Farnlund) was working for Cleminsons Pottery decorating flatware at home at the time, and Moss recommended her to John and Maxine as a very talented artist. She joined them, and the company produced a line of artware dishes, butter pats, trays, and shadowboxes using her decorative designs (the lead glazes used at that time disqualified it for use as dinnerware).

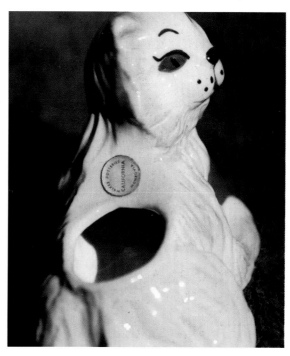

Walker Pottery cat planter with foil sticker. Approximate value $12-15.

Jim recalls that original little stucco building. "My grandfather built that first building. It was never finished. It never had interior walls, except for one sheet of Celotex around the areas where the families lived. My grandparents lived in a room in one corner of it, and mom, dad, and three kids lived in the other end of it, and in the middle was the pottery." The building was about 1500 square feet total, with a 750 square foot concrete apron on the east side where much of the production work was also done.

As the pottery business began to grow, more space was needed. Grimes Pottery had built a Quonset hut near them for manufacturing and shipping. Mrs. Grimes had started the pottery at their home. When they needed more space they built the Quonset hut, but she died not long after and Grimes chose not to continue. When Grimes retired from the business, the building became available and the Hagen-Renaker company occupied it. Several of their employees, most notably Alice Hibarger, who became head decorator at Designers' Workshop, came to work for Hagen-Renaker.

became the tote box of choice for that business. The date flat is about 14" wide by about 20" long and only about 4" deep. It was made of wood. Those boxes came out of the Walker Pottery, which used to be a date packing plant."

The first items to be produced by Hagen-Renaker included dishes and shadowboxes, that were designed by Helen, and flower bowls, designed by Maxine. Then, in 1947, Maxine gave a tour to a Brownie troop and demonstrated the modeling process to the girls. She created a miniature duck with an "insouciant attitude" as John describes it. He was very impressed with it, and this became the first miniature figurine that Hagen-Renaker produced. It was followed by baby ducks, and other animals.

At the January giftware show in 1948, Joe Walker loaned John Renaker a card table in the corner of his showroom, and there Hagen-Renaker set up just a few miniature animals, about a dozen pieces. They sold more than anything else in the show, and that proved to be the turning point for the business.

This Quonset hut housed part of Hagen-Renaker Pottery during its early days. It is now used as a recycling center in Monrovia, California.

With it being located just across a railroad spur from their original building, it gave the Renakers a great opportunity to expand without much investment involved. It also provided an interesting situation for transporting the ware, as Jim explains. "In our early days, that little building became a casting department. The Quonset hut became finishing and decorating. Bill and I used to hand walk the ware and process from casting to the finishing and decorating across the tracks, a few boxes at a time. Then we carried the empty boxes back. The date flat

Bill Nicely, former plant manager, recalls the period well. "Helen did most of the designs at that point, although Maxine did a few. We were never successful at doing those bowls and plates. They were very difficult to do because we tried to do something better. We were hand decorating them all and were doing a nice job of them, but it just wasn't working out. The miniatures lent themselves to our production method in so many ways: they took a lot less material, less kiln space, and were easy to pack and ship."

With resources and equipment still limited, turning to miniatures proved to be a prudent decision for several reasons. Helen also recalls this critical turning point. "We had only one small, top-loading kiln, and somehow usually had grog (the bits of fire brick on the inside of the kiln roof that often fall off when the kiln is fired) on the ware, especially the flat pieces, making them seconds—not very profitable. Maxine made a little duck and a turtle. Those pieces went between the dishes and never got any grog. And they sold. So I tried my hand at animals, I think the first was a clumsy hippo, and we went on from

there and left the dishes behind." The firing was done at first in homemade saggers, a method often used to fire in unmuffled kilns, and the saggers could indeed shed grog. John had learned how to make saggers at Walker Pottery, but it was a laborious and space-wasting technique which was abandoned as soon as good muffle tile and kiln shelves became available again in the post-war period.

Fifty years later, Hagen-Renaker's miniature line has outlasted all other lines for the company, and is still selling strongly.

Early bells, featuring chickens, ducks, and fruit. 2.5" tall, approximate value $25-30.

Oblong console bowl with "Hagen-Renaker Inc./California" inscribed on underside. 16.25" long and 4.5" wide and 2.25" tall. This piece was probably produced much later in Hagen-Renaker's history, since it shows the influence of the Bauer Pottery workers that were hired when that pottery closed. Approximate value $40-45.

Four examples of butter pats. 3.5" round, approximate value $15-18.

Large plate, 8.75" round. John Renaker made the plaster of Paris models for these round plates and other items on the plaster wheel. Helen Perrin Farnlund would then paint the decoration and from that inscribe lines on the master block so that the casting mold would have guidelines for the decorators to follow. It was a cooperative effort between designer (Helen) and mold-maker (John). Approximate value $30-35.

Special order souvenir plates made for Timberline Lodge in Oregon. 5.5" round, approximate value $25-30.

Chrysanthemum oblong plaque. These also came with other flowers, including iris, and two colors of rose. 4" x 5", approximate value $35-40.

Eighteenth century lady and gentleman shadowboxes. There were also sailor boy and sailor girl shadowboxes. 4" x 5", approximate value $35-40.

The initials "AS" found on the back of some of the early items stand for Abra Seeman. She was one of the first decorators hired, and John Renaker says she was one of the best. She initialed some of her work because the company wanted to keep them as prototypes for the other decorators to follow. John recalls her as a very shy and quiet young woman.

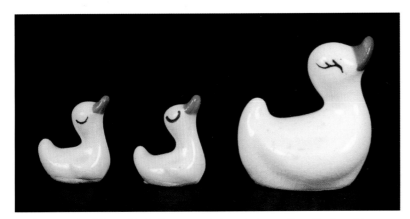

This was the Mama Duck that started the miniature line. Designed by Maxine Renaker, it measures 2" tall. The baby ducks are 1.25" tall. Approximate value for the mama duck is $8-10 and for the baby duck $4-5.

This was a proposal for a new catalog, put together by an artist for the company. Hagen-Renaker decided on the single sheet of paper combined price list/invoice/catalog that they still use today because it was a much more economical format. Note that the artist misspelled "Hagen" throughout the catalog.

2

From Boom to Bust

"I'm told there were 800 potteries in Southern California alone during those war years; you could glaze a lump of clay and someone would buy it!", recalls Helen Perrin Farnlund. It was the late 1940s, and was indeed a boom time for pottery. The majority were small, backyard husband and wife shops. In Monrovia and neighboring towns alone, there were approximately 35 potteries. As the demand continued to grow, more space for Hagen-Renaker production was needed. The company began renting additional industrial buildings within about a six block area in Monrovia.

Around this time, several key employees were added to the rolls, including Bill Mintzer and Joe Griffith, who would run the mold shop, Bill Nicely, future plant manager, and Nell Bortells. The employee roster swelled to about 60 people. The transporting of the ware between buildings for the different phases of processing was still a challenge, as Bill Nicely recalls. "I used to haul the ware from building to building by hand, in the back of Ole Hagen's 1936 Chevrolet, in the back of my 1940 Oldsmobile, or in anything we could get a hold of." John Renaker recalls the Dodge pickup truck that they "bought new around 1952 and fitted with metal shelving opening out from the sides of the bed. It was the first model to have fluid drive which was why we bought it—to avoid any jerky starts. It carried ware on kiln shelves between buildings one or two blocks apart, at no more than five miles per hour. After three years it had about 6000 miles on the odometer and was a total wreck, beyond salvaging."

Bill continues, "After we got pretty much established in groups of buildings, where we did all the production in adjacent buildings, we built ware racks and just moved them on wheeled racks, and that's what we still do today. Some of the racks that I built back in the 1950s are still in use today. We bought the Quonset hut because the owner said that he was going to sell it, and John probably thought that we were going to lose it."

This ware rack was built for moving items around the factory. The ones built for Designers' Workshop were wider with more space between the shelves.

There is absolutely no truth to the rumor that the streets of Monrovia were paved with pieces of pottery from Hagen-Renaker. However, Bill Nicely recalls that he was able to figure out if John Renaker had left to run errands in town by looking for his dusty footprints on the pavement. This photo shows the mold shop.

The demand for the product continued to exceed everyone's expectation. Jim Renaker recounts that incredible period in the company's history. "They went from the depression into the war, and young people were loaded with spending cash, and there wasn't that much around to buy. In those days, brokers would go out to the factories and help unload the kilns for the privilege of buying the merchandise. Brokers would actually be there on Monday mornings waiting for you to open the place up. That thing really mushroomed."

Hagen-Renaker, however, sold directly to stores through agents and to brokers only in the eastern U.S. and in Canada. Their first salesman, Mr. Harper, was an elderly friend of Joe Walker's salesman, and rode with him on his rounds. The association between Joe and Frieda Walker and Moss Renaker was strong, and in 1950 led to the beginning of a new venture. Hagen-Renaker acquired Thomas Pottery and helped start Walker-Renaker Pottery in that facility. The company experimented with making porcelain figurines, an entirely new field for the people involved. Hagen-Renaker's lab man, Brice Whiles, did most of the lab work for this new endeavor. Porcelain fires at a much hotter temperature than pottery, and is harder and more vitreous as a finished product. The first and most popular piece produced in that line actually started out as a Hagen-Renaker miniature, a cow designed by Helen. As the miniature line developed, and the cow no longer fit in, it was discon-

tinued. Two or three years later, Moss took an old mold, cast it in porcelain slip, added a lei of pink and blue flowers and a gold halo, and the "Holy Cow" was born. According to John Renaker, it became the best-selling piece the company ever produced, and within a year there were over 80 people working on that single item. Designer Tom Masterson, who had joined Hagen-Renaker in 1951, created others to go with it, including a bull, named "Bum Steer," a pig, "Pig of my Heart," and others.

The porcelain "Holy Cow." This one is missing the bow that should be on her tail. Approximate value (mint) $15-20.

Another well-known pottery was also located in Monrovia during this period. Josef Originals started in a building on Chestnut Street, next to one of Hagen-Renaker's first plants. Muriel Joseph George's doll line was very successful. Their company was represented by George Good, who was later instrumental in taking the line to Japan. However, the original ideas and designs were conceived and developed in Monrovia, California.

Josef Originals miniature Thoroughbred mare and foal. The mare is 2.5" tall, and the foal is 1" tall. Approximate values are $12-15 for the mare and $10-12 for the foal.

Josef Originals adorable ponies. This whimsical style was also typical of her other animals and dolls. White pony is 2.75" tall and the black pony is 2.25" tall. Approximate values are $15-20 for the white pony and $12-15 for the black one.

John Renaker was always looking for ways to expand and invest. During World War II, he had become friends with John Bennett while the two worked for North American Aviation. After the war, the two men remained in touch. When Arcadia Ceramics became available, the two went into partnership and bought it. Among other items, Arcadia had produced a line of salt cellars which the new owners continued, but in miniature form. Some of these were so small that, as Bill Nicely recalls, "They wouldn't hold enough salt to salt your sandwich." The sets were designed for the collector's market. Their sole reason for being was novelty and they included such improbable items as an iron and ironing board, a cow jumping over the moon, a dish of pancakes and a syrup bottle, and many more. None were more than 1.5" tall. Unfortunately, miniature salt and pepper shakers were something that the Japanese could produce very well, so Arcadia Ceramics went the way of most of the potteries in California. John Bennett returned to his job at North American Aviation. Meanwhile, John Renaker sold the old Thomas Pottery plant (Walker-Renaker had ceased operations) to Howard

Johnson, the previous owner of Arcadia Ceramics, who used it for a new business that produced aluminum castings in plaster molds. It was highly successful and Johnson induced John Bennett to leave North American Aviation and work for him as a designer and estimator.

Millesan Drews also created the Keikis (Hawaiian Children). Although Hagen-Renaker held the license for them, they were never put into full production. They were later licensed to be produced in Japan

Examples of the tiny salt cellars made by Arcadia. Note the phrase on top of the spool of thread that reads "No silver threads among the gold." The spool of thread came with a golden thimble. Both pieces have only one hole for the salt to dispense from. The spool is 1" tall, the log 0.5" tall. Approximate value of each is $12-15.

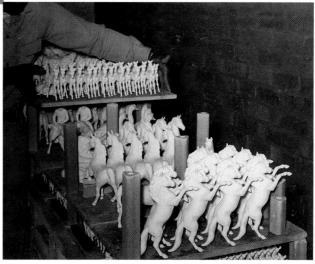

Finished Designers' Workshop horses headed for a final firing in the large kiln.

The pixie figurines that Millesan Drews created were made in two parts, so that the top and bottom of the pixies were interchangeable. This allowed for numerous combinations, creating interesting poses. All of the ones produced by Hagen-Renaker had golden slippers. Approximate value $45-50. Toadstool measures 3" tall and has an approximate value of $15-20.

The wooden base that the jumping pixie is mounted on is not original, but was created so that he could be displayed upright.

The early 1950s were a period of rapid growth. In 1952, the Designers' Workshop line was started, which was run by Bill Nicely and Nell Bortells. Other endeavors included a line of dolls (Dominique dolls), copper enamel jewelry by Marsha Best, and the pixie line and Keiki figures of Millesan Drews. Don Winton of Twin Winton Pottery designed pieces for the miniatures modeled on characters from the just released Disney film Lady and the Tramp. He also designed cookie jars (a new departure for Hagen-Renaker) in the form of well known Disney characters such as Dumbo the elephant, Figaro the cat, and the Practical Pig. Don also designed Snow White and Nell Bortells did the companion Seven Dwarfs for the Designers' Workshop line. Don

Winton designed miniature versions of Mickey Mouse and Pluto, Donald Duck and his nephews, and Peter Pan, while Helen did characters from Fantasia. During that period Martha Armstrong joined the group at Designers' Workshop, designing abstract animals to be produced in polished stoneware bisque, and also realistic human figures. Suzy Singer produced a line of small Romanesque putti figurines for porcelain production at Walker-Renaker. A wartime émigré from Vienna, her forte had been and continued to be the production of individual clay pieces, often commissioned by and sold to patrons of her Hollywood studio. She was highly respected as a ceramic artist and Maxine studied with her for several months in the early 1950s. But her pieces could not be adapted to mold production without losing their distinctive character and so were never put into full production.

Lady and Tramp were sculpted by Don Winton. After the Disney license agreement lapsed, the molds were still used to make dogs that did not have the intricate designs of the Disney pieces. Lady measures 1.75" tall and Tramp is 2.25" tall. Approximate value for Lady is $45-60 and for Tramp $125-140.

Lady and Tramp's puppies Fluffy, Scamp, Ruffles, and Scooter. All are just under 1" tall and have an approximate value of $40-50.

...and NOW *Hagen-Renaker presents...*

CERAMIC MINIATURES

JOCK 75¢

SI 75¢

AM 75¢

PEDRO 70¢

TRUSTY 80¢

DACHSIE 60¢

Lady 80¢

Tramp 1.00

SCOOTER 50¢

SCAMP 50¢

FLUFFY 50¢

RUFFLES 50¢

FROM THE CAST OF

WALT DISNEY'S Lady AND THE Tramp

In 1956, a 40,000 square foot building was constructed on Shamrock Street to bring all of the various production stages under one roof. In order to qualify for the Small Business Administration loan to build the big building, Hagen-Renaker had to stop hiring people and let attrition trim the payroll down to 300 people. This number of employees then increased to more than 320, the highest figure ever attained. The move to the large building made economic sense because at the time Hagen-Renaker was paying rent for about eleven separate facilities. The building included five acres of land, so the fledging nursery business could also be expanded. It was a glorious time to be in this new, state of the art facility, but the company did not sell the old Quonset hut. As Bill Nicely recalls, "We kept the Quonset hut kind of as a keepsake, which was a good thing, because we needed it about four years later."

The new factory Hagen-Renaker built in 1956 that Jim Renaker described as being as large as a supermarket. This is a recent photo taken of that building.

Meanwhile, during this period until about 1960, Hagen-Renaker began a steady hunt for new models and new ideas. With the foreign competition making similar products that were cheaper, there was a constant effort in place to make new and different things that could not be copied. The Little Horribles line was introduced in 1958 and was an immediate success. Two lines of wall plaques were tried; one was a rock-type form, and one was mounted on wood panels, in a mosaic style. The black bisque line also emerged during this period, using a special enameling technique. But by the late 1950s the Japanese competition eroded sales badly, and in 1960 Hagen-Renaker closed down operations for several months.

Horse rock plaques, designed by Maureen Love. Large one measures 21.5" wide, smaller ones are 16" tall. Approximate values $150-175 large one and $130-150 each for the smaller ones. Other rock plaque designs included fish, butterflies, and deer.

Opposite page: Sales brochure promoting the Lady and the Tramp series.

Jack plaque, measures 12" by 18". This set was made of several parts then assembled on a wooden panel. Made for only a short time in 1959, they are considered very rare.

Queen plaque.

Mosaic of ship with seagulls, mounted on wooden panel. Very rare.

King plaque. There was also a set of two Geisha girls made this same way and the same size, one with a fan and one without. All are considered very rare.

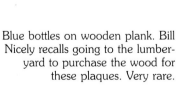

Blue bottles on wooden plank. Bill Nicely recalls going to the lumber-yard to purchase the wood for these plaques. Very rare.

Examples of the black bisque line of figurines. The fox is 3.75" tall and was designed by Tom Masterson. The elephant was designed by Will Climes and is 3" tall. Their approximate values are $40-45 for the fox and $50-60 for the elephant.

Black bisque dog with removable head, designed by Helen Perrin Farnlund. Measuring 3" by 9.5", this is one of the largest black bisque pieces. Approximate value $100-125.

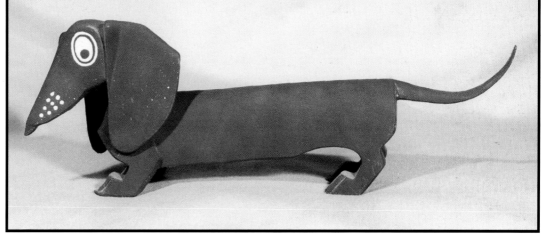

The black bisque zebra and horse were both designed by Maureen Love. The zebra is 5.3" tall and the horse is 4.5" tall. The approximate value for each is $80-100.

Display photo taken by Hagen-Renaker for their sales staff to take into the field for prospective buyers. Photos like these were often made of prototype figures before they were in the production run and decorated by the best decorators on staff. This circus tent set up was not available to purchase, but the individual animals were.

The worst part of all was telling the 200 or so employees of Hagen-Renaker still on the payroll that the company was closing and that they were being let go. The only ones left were Bill Nicely, Jim Renaker, and John Renaker who drew no pay but split whatever they could collect from the sale of equipment and remaining pottery inventory. The talented team of designers that had been assembled were scattered to other endeavors, the dedicated staff was released, and the pottery faced its darkest time ever.

Jim remembers the period well. "The thing began to hit the skids. As it happens, we probably would have been better off staying with all those rented buildings, because we could have shrunk with the times. As it was, we stuck with that big building and a huge mortgage till we couldn't stand it anymore. Then we finally had to close it and sell it. I finally found a guy who had an expanding business. He was making the main rotor blades for the HU-1 helicopter, the Huey, for use in Vietnam. It was beautifully suited for him; the lighting was all at the right level and everything. Once the mortgage was gone, we had capital, so we could move back into the Quonset hut and start up again."

Designers Nell Bortells, Helen Perrin Farnlund, and Maureen Love joined forces briefly with mold men Bill Mintzer and Joe Griffith to purchase McAfee's (MAC uh FEEZ) Pottery. As Helen recalls, "We tried. It was a pottery that had been run by people called McAfee, and we just kept the name. It didn't last long; we didn't make very much money. We were making ashtrays and birdhouses, and bowls, and such. No little animals." When this endeavor failed, they sold the company and each went their own way.

Designers' Workshop employees group photo taken December 2, 1954. Front row: 1st position Penny Lieber, 2nd Nell Bortells, 3rd Lucias Lewis, 4th Ole Hagen, 5th Hugh Paris, 6th Don Meyer, 7th Bob Bouch, 8th John Renaker, 9th Mary Renaker, 10th Bill Nicely, 11th Margaret Ware. Third row: 4th position Maxine Renaker, 6th Maureen Love, 9th Bonnie Banker, 19th Marlys Klepper. Fourth row: 2nd position Ann Baker, 14th Lucia Payne.

3

Recovery and Beyond

The company returned to the Quonset hut that it had once outgrown. The dream of a pottery was kept alive by Bill Nicely, Maxine Renaker, and Phil Leitsch, Hagen-Renaker's salesman for the entire state of California. According to Mary Renaker, her mother said "'This is going to be a good business again.' and it really boosted morale in that old Quonset hut. She showed up every day and even put me to work there after school at age 14. She had a fire in her belly and she wasn't going to let that company go. She and Bill and Lucia Payne worked it up from the bottom again. And Bill gets tons of credit here too." Bill put together a mailing which brought in some business, and sales began to climb once more.

Moving from the 40,000 square foot building into the 2,000 square foot Quonset hut was difficult. John Renaker used the money from the sale of the Walker-Renaker plant to buy ten acres of industrial land in San Dimas. There, with Jim's help, he relocated the nursery which had been started on a lot next to his friend Olle Ollson's nursery in Monrovia. When space was tight in the Quonset hut, the molds for the large Designers' Workshop animals were moved to the San Dimas property. Later (1962) Jim supervised the construction of a new plant for the pottery and they were stored inside an outbuilding. Many of those molds are still there today, pretty much the way Bill and Jim put them years ago.

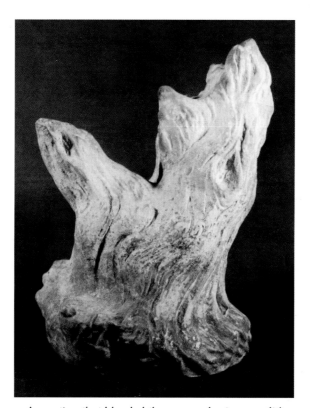

A creation that blended the nursery business and the pottery business was the Living Tree. It was a planter shaped like a tree. A plant could be grown inside it and the leaves would poke out of the openings as the plant grew. These varied in size and style.

Some of the Designers' Workshop horse molds in storage at the San Dimas factory.

To the degree the building code allowed, the new building used greenhouse technology. The bright, airy interior conditions are ideal for the artists and other employees. The kilns are outside, in sheds adjacent to the building, which makes it easier to keep the buildings cool in the summer.

The Hagen-Renaker factory, San Dimas, California.

Sign at the main entrance to the Hagen-Renaker property.

When Bauer Pottery closed, Hagen-Renaker absorbed some of their employees for the production of nursery pots. With the expertise of the Bauer designers, mold makers, and jiggermen, they were able to produce a line of bonsai pots, sand jars, and jardinieres. In the pot production process, great big jardiniere pots would be turned on pottery wheels to finish them. This is called jiggering. Bill Nicely recalls that, "We never did get a designer from Bauer Pottery, except for the mold maker Tracy. But he just threw them on the wheel." None of the Bauer workers helped in the Hagen-Renaker figurine line.

A friend of the Renakers, Doc Fields, was facing problems with his company, Roselane Pottery. The California freeway system was taking over his property. He sold the land to Caltran, then was able to lease it back for about four years to continue producing his pottery, until they actually needed to demolish the building. To help him market his ware, Phil Leitsch, one of the Hagen-Renaker salesmen, stepped in. Phil liked the Roselane line, so he convinced Hagen-Renaker to sell it for Doc. A small inventory of the Roselane products was kept in the Hagen-Renaker shipping department, but because it was shipped from there, the Hagen-Renaker oval California state sticker was placed on the items before they left. After about four years, the freeway took his building and Doc retired. He passed away shortly after that.

This Roselane owl has the small oval state of California Hagen-Renaker foil sticker on its back. The owl measures 3.5" tall and has an approximate value of $10.

Meanwhile, in 1969 Jim Renaker and his wife Freya left for Mexico to start their own pottery business, Ceramica Regalmex. The name "Regalmex" was a composite of "Renaker," "Galvan," Jim's Mexican partner, and "Mexico." In 1974, Susan Nikas, John and Maxine's oldest daughter, took over the supervision of the nursery in San Dimas and became secretary/treasurer for the company. For four years she commuted from her home in Long Beach.

Over the next 10 to 15 years, the miniature line flourished, but the Designers' Workshop line was trimmed. It was finally discontinued in Fall, 1972, but was briefly revived in 1975. John Renaker explains it this way. "We were forever looking for ways to give the designers more scope to express their talents. That was why the new line started in 1952 was called 'Designers' Workshop.' Although it had some notable commercial successes—for example Maureen Love's horses and Tom Masterson's climbing cat—it often failed to show a profit. Nonetheless, it was almost a barometer of the company's success. Whenever Hagen-Renaker prospered, Designers' Workshop, or some line like it, was revived or reinvented."

In 1978, after 30 years of service, Bill Nicely retired, and Susan took over the running of the pottery. Then a new chapter began. Maxine Renaker heard from former employee Robyn Sikking and her daughter Laurilyn

This large Freeman-McFarlin Siamese cat has an oval sticker on it from the El Monte, California plant. The company moved to San Marcos around 1970. The cat is 14" tall and the approximate value is $30-40.

Burson that the Freeman-McFarlin Pottery Company in San Marcos was for sale. Always looking for ways to expand Hagen-Renaker, Maxine and John investigated it, then brought the decision to the board of trustees for a decision. The result was that in 1980 Hagen-Renaker bought the Freeman-McFarlin plant from International Multifoods, a conglomerate that had purchased that pottery and had been trying unsuccessfully to run the little company from Milwaukee.

This cute adult bird was made in the San Marcos plant of Freeman-McFarlin. Note the rectangular sticker under its wing that indicates the new location of the factory. The bird stands 4" tall and has an approximate value of $20-25.

Jim Renaker returned from Mexico to rejoin the family business. For about the first year and a half, Hagen-Renaker continued to produce some of the Freeman-McFarlin pieces, but gradually those were phased out and Designers' Workshop pieces were substituted into the line. At first, Eric Brazel, the son-in-law of the Renakers, was the plant manager and Mary Renaker was the national sales manager. After three years, Eric and Mary returned to their own pottery business.

This sales poster from 1985 shows the Designers' Workshop line, which still included some of the Freeman-McFarlin molds. The large white horse on the top shelf is 12" tall.

DESIGNER'S WORKSHOP
520 CARMEL STREET — SAN MARCOS, CALIFORNIA 92069 — (619) 744-1544

Since the Designers' Workshop molds had been in storage for so many years, they needed to be reworked, or even replaced. Jim Renaker recalls that "for use at the San Marcos factory, virtually every one of the H-R molds were remade. Almost everything was a remake, because those original blocks were made in castable epoxy resin. A lot of it was just too used up to use again. So in most cases we got the best mold off of it we could, and made a wax piece on it. Once you've got the wax pretty close,

it's not like modeling it from scratch. It's what we refer to as a clean-up." Then a new mold can be made. "In the San Marcos factory, a lot of the larger Designers' Workshop pieces came back. We remodeled the cowboy rider and horse. Originally it was cast all in one piece. We separated the rider from the horse in San Marcos, and it made a more interesting piece out of it. We got more details under the pant legs and so forth. It looks the same in a picture, but it really was a remodel at San Marcos."

Here is an example of an animal that changed appearance when the mold was reworked. On the right is the older version of the doe Patience and on the left is the newer version that was done in the San Marcos plant. The older version was designed by Tom Masterson and is 3.75" tall. The newer version is 4" tall and was redone by Helen Perrin Farnlund. The older one has an approximate value of $30-35 and the newer one $25-30.

The cowboy horse and rider as it was produced in the San Marcos factory. It measures 8.5" tall. Earlier horses also came in bay (dark brown), black, and chestnut. The older versions from the 50s and 60s are worth approximately $450-500, the newer ones from the 80s are worth $200-225.

Meanwhile, designers Helen Perrin Farnlund, Maureen Love, and Nell Bortells came back to work for Hagen-Renaker, this time with special arrangements to work out of their homes. But the San Marcos factory venture was not to last. In 1986, the property was sold and the company regrouped in the San Dimas plant, making only miniatures once again. Jim headed for Mexico to open another pottery company, Loza Electrica, with his son Eric. Bill Nicely returned to work for Hagen-Renaker in 1988, as a part time technical consultant. The San Dimas location was expanded to six buildings.

Miniatures continue to be the mainstay of the company. According to Hagen-Renaker dealer Terri Benton, the total line is kept to around 230 items with new items being introduced and a similar number of pieces being retired twice a year, in January and July. In recent years, the Specialties line has been created to provide interesting figurines that are slightly larger than the miniatures. This line has featured horses, fish, fairies, wild animals, musical frogs and other pieces. Beginning in 1993, approximately every 18 months a horse model in the 5-6" scale has been made available in the Collectors' Series. These horses have all been sculpted by Maureen Love and have helped to satisfy the collectors who long for the days of the Designers' Workshop horses.

John Renaker officially retired as Chairman of the Board and President of the Corporation on March 31, 1996, although he continues to look in on the nursery business, now located near his and Maxine's home in Encinitas. Susan Nikas carries on the family tradition to develop new talent and create new items. She explains, "It is, of course, a team effort to work out the practical tasks of transforming the artist's sculpture into a piece that can be mass-produced. It starts with our wonderful designers, Helen Perrin Farnlund, Maureen Love, Bob McGuinness, Nell Bortells, and several other artists. Our master mold maker, Pedro Armenta and his assistant Jim Dawson work out the tooling on the piece. Then we begin to work out the colors; what the base color will be and then what colors will be added to give the effect that we want. Mary Lou Salas, my production manager, works very closely with me on this. I cannot emphasize too much that there is a group effort to put out the very best piece we can."

This giraffe was recently sculpted by Maureen Love. It measures 3.25" tall and has an approximate value of $18-20.

A delicate Monarch butterfly sculpted by Maureen Love for the specialties line. It stands 4" tall and the approximate value is $15-20.

The girl and pony figure is part of the specialties line. It was designed by Robert McGuinness and stands 2.75" tall. There are two versions; a blonde girl and a brunette girl. The blonde version is older and worth slightly more. Approximate value $18-25.

This Guinea pig was sculpted for the miniature line by Kristina Lucas, who is best known for her horse sculptures. Her company Lucas Studio and Pour Horse, which also features her horses, are located in California. This Guinea pig is 1" tall and the approximate value is $5.

Panda Papa was designed by Shi Yi Chen and measures 1.8" tall. He is a current piece with an approximate value of $5-8.

The lynx was a part of the miniature line and was available both with and without the base. It was designed by Robert McGuinness and is 1.12" tall. The approximate value is $8-10.

This lovable Saint Bernard is a current piece in the miniature line. It was designed by Robert McGuinness and stands 1.8" tall. Approximate value is $5-6.

A miniature howling coyote designed by Maureen Love. It is large for the miniature line, measuring 2.5" tall. It has an approximate value of $6-8.

Adorable set of raccoons designed by Robert McGuinness. Papa raccoon on the fence has his full body on the backside, out of view. Papa with fence is 2.25" tall and the baby on the ground is 1.25" tall. There is also a mama with the set, up on her hind legs. Approximate value for papa is $6-8, and for the baby $3-5.

Jamboree is a bit more stylized than other horses designed by Maureen Love. It came in three colors, gray, tan, and bay (the color shown) all with Appaloosa patterns. These were decorated by Laurilyn Burson, and numbered and signed by the designer. Issued in 1993, it had a limited run of 262 pieces. It measures 5" and has an approximate value of $120-130.

Encore the Arabian was the second in the Collectors' Series, issued in 1994. It came in white, bay, chestnut, and dapple gray (the color shown). It was signed and numbered by Maureen Love the designer and only 418 were produced. Measuring 5.5" tall, the approximate value is $200-225, with the dapple gray ones being worth the most.

Third in the Collectors' Series was Tria, the Morgan mare. She was produced in late 1995-early 1996 in a limited run of 200. She was available in both palomino and bay (color shown) and stands 4" tall. Her base also bears the signature of Maureen Love and the production number. Approximate value $110-125.

Finally, Quartet the Quarter Horse rounds out this series. Still currently available in an open edition of 1,000, this horse is produced in white, bay, chestnut, and dark gray (color shown). Mounted on a base with the signature of Maureen Love and the number of the piece, it stands 5" tall and retails for $100 from the company.

4

John & Maxine Renaker

John Renaker worked as a librarian at UCLA, from 1938 to 1941, but while he enjoyed the work, he found that he could not support his family—particularly after the twins, David and Susan were born in 1940—on a junior librarian's salary. With the idea of getting a job in one of the war plants then expanding furiously, he went to night school for two years, studying mathematics and engineering drawing, and soon after Pearl Harbor went to work at North American Aviation as a draftsman. He worked on the P-51 Mustang, which was quite a famous aircraft.

At the end of the war, he went to work for Walker Pottery. His mother Moss Renaker worked there through the war, so she helped him get a job there so he could learn the trade. He blunged clay, milled engobes, blended glazes, worked in shipping and receiving, and when not otherwise occupied, concocted systems for improving production which he urged Joe Walker to try. Some of them worked (a method for drying the molds in place by using waste heat from the kilns, and air pressure systems for moving slip from blunger to the casting area) and he used the ideas later in his own plant.

Jim comments, "These shops were traditionally mostly women workers, so one or two men in the place were about all they could tolerate, I guess. So the men ended up doing all the heavy work. It was the first time I'd ever seen him with muscles."

Then in 1946 John moved his family into the building built by his father-in-law Ole Hagen in Monrovia and the pottery business began. In the early days, it took much hard work and effort, even to the point of building his own kilns for the pottery. Maxine did most of the hiring, according to John. Also, John further explains, "Around that time we were making a miscellany of artware pieces and keeping careful track of sales, particularly write-in orders and salesman's records, for clues to the kind of items store owners were able to sell easily. The number one best seller was Maxine's little duck family, and I asked the decorators: 'Does anyone want to try making a small animal?' Helen said she would like to try and produced a hippo. When Maxine saw it she said, 'Oh! That's far better than anything I could do!' Actually the pieces Maxine made were all successes. The baby skunk in particular (it eventually became the mama skunk) stayed in production for forty years. But she was right in her immediate recognition of Helen's talent. Within a year Helen was designing pieces that could be made in two-piece molds that none of us had believed possible. Ever after we decided to put baby ducks with Maxine's first miniature duck and the customers applauded the idea, all animals had to have babies."

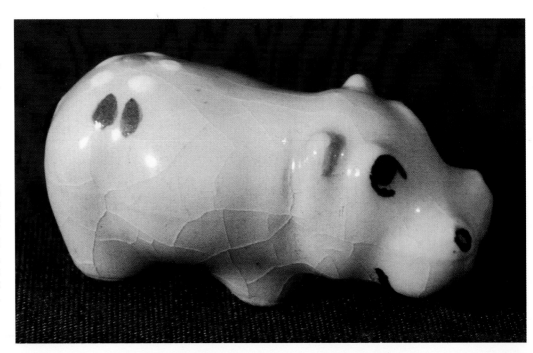

This hippo mama was designed by Maxine Renaker, and also has a companion baby hippo that is similar in appearance. It stands 1" tall, and can be found with and without a flower on its rump. Approximate value $10-15, with the flower version being worth more.

Maxine produced a variety of skunks in the early years. They are the textured mama skunk (1.25"), the skunk papa (2"), the skunk mama (1.8"), another skunk mama (1"), and the skunk baby (.75"). Values range from $3 for the smallest to $15 for the largest.

Throughout Hagen-Renaker's history, John served the crucial roll of mentor, friend, boss, and critic to help nurture and develop the product and the talent of those involved with it. An example of this is shown in a story told by Bill Nicely, talking about the Designers' Workshop climbing cat. "It was a very, very popular item in Designers' Workshop. Tom Masterson designed it. When John Renaker first saw it, the climbing cat had both feet on the ground. He was the one who asked Tom to move the legs so that it was actually climbing like it is, up against the surface. That was done at The House That Jack Built, a popular little restaurant around the corner. I can remember sitting there and looking at the model with John and Tom, and John not liking it. John was the main critic, and he was the person who was responsible for all of the innovations as far as design was concerned. When John looked at something, he could pretty well tell that it was going to go, and make criticisms that were beneficial."

Helen Perrin Farnlund further explains, "John usually requested what he wanted, and left it up to us to come up with something. He is one of the kindest and most generous of men. I think all the employees felt very loyal. If one wasn't doing well, rather than dismiss her, John found a different job she could do."

John Renaker smoking his annual cigar at the mold shop Christmas party while Bill Mintzer and Helen Perrin (now Farnlund) watch.

This climbing cat was an example of how John Renaker would look at a piece and make suggestions to improve it. This Siamese cat measures 6.5" long and the approximate value is $30-40.

Martha Armstrong Hand shares her memories of the Renakers. "Extremely friendly. We had the best impression of Mr. and Mrs. Renaker. They were sweet people. Very strict, you wouldn't cross him, but understanding and had a sense of humor, and oh, dear, I love those people! They are a wonderful couple. My children would visit there, we all visited in their home. We were friends. Also, the fact that he had me stay in the mold shop and learn it, now that in itself is absolutely wonderful. What a sensible idea! Can you imagine? For a designer to go through the process of mold making, to understand it."

Another designer, Maureen Love, also has praise for John. "He's a great guy. He is a good critic. He has a very good eye, in other words. He pretty much let us alone, for the most part."

The gingham dog is one of the very few pieces that John Renaker is responsible for designing. This adorable dog is 2.5" tall and also came in pink with white polka dots. The color of the dots changes on the other side of the dog, and there are stitches up the front just like on a stuffed animal. This dog is very rare.

One of the few animals designed by Maxine Renaker, this sheep was only made for a short time in the late 40s. It stands 2.1" tall and is considered rare.

Maxine's role in the pottery business lessened while raising their four children. But, as daughter Mary Renaker recalls, even in the worst of times, "Dad had my mom who kept the pottery business going and refused to give up or let it go. She never doubted my father's abilities and was ready to take on any adventure with him. Dad was, and is, always positive, and his reaction to the cave-in at H-R was to begin carving up our backyard on Hillcrest in Monrovia, for the nursery business. This was his second attempt at business, and as you know, it is still going."

John noted: "It is important to understand the degree to which Japanese competition influenced decisions in the decade of the 1950s. At first we added new items and opened new sales territories in order to expand, but soon it seemed that we had to do that in order not to lose ground. Before long every state in the union was covered, and while we added dozens of new pieces and dropped those whose turnover rates had slowed, still sales began to flag as the Japanese made inroads with copies at cheaper prices. We responded by producing entire new lines: first Designers' Workshop, then Walker-Renaker porcelain, then Millicent Drew's Keiki figurines, and then Disney merchandise. We thought at the time that we would gain a respite by taking shelter under the Disney copyright umbrella, and at first it seemed that we had found the answer. But to our astonishment, the Disney pieces did not sell well in the stores. While Disney merchandise always sold well as toys, it was evidently not well-suited to the niche of fragile pottery miniatures. At that point we took another tack, and began production of larger items that would be harder for the Japanese to undersell because of higher shipping costs. We produced large wall-mounted pieces—some in the form of rock slabs with incised designs reminiscent of prehistoric cave art, and others made of flat pottery sections fitted together like jigsaw puzzles and decorated with bright jewelry enamels. These were inspired by Tarot card designs, Japanese prints (Geishas), cubist art, and were mounted on polished wooden plaques. When the old Bauer Pottery, a Los Angeles landmark, quit business, we hired some of its key employees and tried to produce some of its more popular planters and also added some of our own design. Meanwhile, the miniatures remained the mainstay of the business. Even as sales declined, it provided the funds for the experimental ventures. The only new line that showed a profit—the Little Horribles designed by Nell Bortells—was produced in the same sizes and made use of the same techniques as the miniatures.

In the end, the question of what to do about Japanese competition became critical. Our sales manager, George Good, thought that since we couldn't beat 'em we ought to join 'em. For more than a year we explored the possibility. It appeared less inviting with every passing month. Finally we split with Good and Company, and with no sales force and a big plant we could no longer afford, shut up shop."

Youngest daughter Mary has a great story regarding George Good. She recounts "George Good mellowed in his later years, and I remember him leaning over a table in our booth in the LA Gift Show about 1982 to say hello amid the busy crowd, and then to say to me, 'You know your father is the closest thing to a genius I have ever known.'"

John was able to take an idea, develop it, and push it to a new level. The papa deer issued in 1949 exemplified that. First, there was the lying fawn, a simple piece cast in brown slip. Next, the mama deer took the art of making four-legged animals in two-piece molds further than the company had so far managed to do. Finally, the papa deer, with separate legs and antlers which no one but John thought would be possible. It took excellent design (Helen), new mold making technology (Bill Mintzer and low melting temperature metal alloys), and especially skilled casters and finishers. The piece was a success, and continues to sell well after 40 years in production. John concludes, "When people asked what I did for a living I showed them that piece, even though all I had to do with it was cheer from the side lines." While enjoying retirement, John still strolls to the nursery facility and checks in daily.

Mary comments, "My mom was one of the first 'grays' to go back to college and was very popular with teachers and students. She had a ball at Pasadena City College, and they quickly shooed her into LA State University where she got her degree in English and then her teaching credential. Not because she needed the money, but she needed the mental stimulation."

Finally, in the postlog to Maxine's Book *One Lucky Kid* Richard Pizzoferrato, her computer instructor, comments on "Maxine's taking up computing at age 76" and being "responsible for getting her whole family into computing." He goes on to say, "I truly admire Maxine's energy, spirit and great accomplishments." Richard's comments about John were that he "was by far, brighter than I had ever been. He was knowledgeable, well spoken, considerate and made me feel real and appreciated. This was John's way."

Miniature papa deer, designed by Helen Perrin Farnlund. It measures 2.75" tall and came in dark and light brown. Approximate value is $12-15 for dark brown and $5-6 for light brown (pictured).

5

Jim Renaker

Jim is the oldest of the four children of John and Maxine Renaker, born in 1937. His involvement with Hagen-Renaker spans several years, with breaks for other ventures. According to Jim, "As far as when I went to work for Hagen-Renaker, we all lived in the little pottery building in the beginning. I worked at whatever a little kid could do. I remember straining slip. You have to push slip through a very fine screen with a rubber spatula in order to get the grit out of it. I did that. They started to pay me a little bit in 1947; I got a dime an hour. By 1949, when California had a minimum wage, they had to give me a quarter. Then, of course, I stayed with it. There was only one summer that I didn't work for the pottery."

Eventually Hagen-Renaker took over a Quonset hut across a railroad spur from the original building, and there was a lot more work for Jim to do. "In those early days, my grandfather had a place in the lumberyard, a saw shed in the lumberyard, where he and I worked. I worked after school every day in the afternoon and he was there most of the day, every day. The lumberyard people just roughed out tables for us, and we banged them together with nails. Spent years doing that; building workstations and little tables, and casting tables, and racks for molds. Just all sorts of wood furniture. It was 1951-1953, it was a steady process, growing rapidly." He also recalls that the mold shop was "where I spent most of my time when I wasn't banging nails."

As the company grew, Jim helped set up the facilities in several rented buildings around Monrovia, and eventually the question came up whether or not it was time to build their own building. When asked by his father if he had any intention of following along in the trade, at the age of 16 or 17, Jim's reply was, "I've got nothing better to do." And that's what he did. The large brick building was built, which Jim describes as "a large supermarket building, a little over an acre of building." According to Mary Renaker, Jim also attended UCLA. There he met Freya and at age 19 married her.

Jim was continuously involved in the growing and shrinking of the pottery, through good times then through bad. The firing of the entire staff in 1961-1962, the sale of the brick building in Monrovia, the move to San Dimas, and the eventual purchase and start up of San Marcos were all events that he was instrumental in. In between, he spent 19 or 20 years away from the company.

This photo was in the 1965 San Dimas "Decade of Progress" report. Shown in the photo from left to right are building inspector Bob Smith, Jim Renaker, John Renaker, and Bill Nicely.

As Jim explains, "I started a pottery business in Tecate, Mexico. Ceramica RegalMex. It was my first company, and it was successful. I had a partner named Pilar Galvan (who according to Mary worked in their dad's nursery at the time). I made terra-cotta planters, tile, and stuff like that for the nursery business for years and years. Have you ever heard of the Chia Pet™? Well, I started it. I just made the parts, but I don't know anything about the details of the business. It's gotten to be a big deal. I sold that when I sold my business. Maureen also made a few things for me. She was freelance at the time, and I had her do a few designs. She did a lying down pig, which we made a little planter out of, a tortoise, and some other good little things."

Jim returned to Hagen-Renaker when the San Marcos plant was purchased in 1980. "Basically, I wanted to do that because I wanted to make pretty things. I was to go back and take part in that. I was to be a teacher of mold making." But working with the crew in the San Marcos plant Jim quickly realized that "I didn't have to do anything but just stand back and help," as Rich Steckman "already had it down pat." Since the building was full of Freeman-McFarlin inventory, Jim found a buyer for it and sold and delivered 20 tons of pottery to a contact at Williamsburg Pottery, in Williamsburg, Virginia. Slowly, the Freeman-McFarlin line was phased out, and the Hagen-Renaker Designers' Workshop pieces were substituted.

When the San Marcos plant closed, Jim was eager to find a new challenge. Hagen-Renaker shrank back to just the San Dimas facility again, and Jim felt it was time to move on. He returned to Mexico and started Loza Electrica with his son Eric (EJ) and with designer Jose Castro. He describes Jose as "more of a general mold maker than a pottery mold maker. I taught him all the pottery stuff, and he's very good at that. But he also does wax, metals, silver, and gold. He's a very talented guy."

In 1998, Loza closed its doors for business. Jim had worked for Hagen-Renaker from age 10 to 30, then from 1980-86, and between that time was self employed in pottery in Mexico. He made many friends among the staff of Hagen-Renaker and speaks fondly and respectfully of the designers, the mold men, and the others he's had the opportunity to work with.

Pottery Chia Pet. Note on the belly of the animal is etched the word "Mexico." This one stands about 5" tall and the approximate value is $6-10.

This handsome Loza Arabian Stallion closely resembles the Hagen-Renaker Arabian stallion Nataf, but in miniature. Available in white or gray, this horse measures 3.25" and the approximate value is $10-15.

Trotting 5.5" sport horse mounted on a ceramic base. Most of the larger Loza horses are on bases. Approximate value $25-30.

Loza duck measuring 2" tall. Approximate value $4-6.

6

Susan Lee Nikas

When it was time for John and Maxine Renaker to retire from the pottery business, they were able to turn the reins over to their daughter Susan Nikas who has been running Hagen-Renaker ever since. Susan attributes their continuing success to "Luck, and good designs, and very good employees. We have had good designers and we have done our best to translate their artistry into mass produced products."

Her first exposure to the business was at the research and development division with her twin David in Newport Beach, under the direction of her brother Jim Renaker. "This was an effort to mass-produce the wall plaques (pseudo mosaics) by using epoxy molds made with drill presses. I think as much as anything it was an attempt by my dad to turn his teenagers into entrepreneurs. My older brother fired me and I remember that my dad was very proud of his son's toughness!"

Susan came into the family business in 1974, filling various roles. "I started working for Hagen-Renaker in 1974 during my spring vacation from teaching (I was an 8th grade history teacher at the time). My mother was concerned because the family wasn't very involved in the business. My initial duties were to learn the office so that I could be 'controller' of the Corporation. For someone who had never even balanced her checkbook at that point in time, it was a bit of a challenge. One of the first things I was taught, by our outside bookkeepers, was to balance Hagen-Renaker's checkbook. (Something I can still do when I have to do so.)"

"I began running the Nursery Division soon after I came to work when my dad put me in charge of setting up a 'green book' (daily accounting) for the nursery. The nursery manager got so disgusted with my questioning of his figures that he quit and I got the job by default."

"My mother and I took over running the pottery in 1978 when Bill Nicely decided that he wanted to take early retirement. He had been working for the company for 31 years at that point and was 'burned out.' My mother and father had moved to Encinitas in 1972 and she was commuting. So, we bought her a trailer next door and she stayed there three or four nights a week. She would come up on Monday and go home on Friday. Needless to say this became onerous over time, and

by 1980 I was pretty much running the place, but with a very active and involved Board of Directors."

"In 1981, we bought the Freeman-McFarlin plant in San Marcos and my mom, dad, Jim and Mary along with my brother-in-law Eric Brazel became very involved with that. I helped a bit on the bookkeeping end of it. In 1986, we gave up on that. My dad did not retire from running the nursery until 1996 and even now, he helps me by advising our nursery manager, Juan Barajas. Except for advice, he has allowed me to run the pottery since the early eighties. He officially retired as chairman of the Board and president of the Corporation on March 31, 1996."

Nell Bortells comments that "Sue has done a magnificent job. She has developed a crew that really does wonderful work. It's just a whole different world, but I think Sue has done just a magnificent job at the pottery. She's really brought new life into it. I think her folks are extremely proud of her. I've known her since she was a pup. I think she's a terrific gal." Helen Perrin Farnlund adds, "Susan is a very bright young woman. She's gotten quite inventive and has gotten a crew that's able to do things and likes a challenge. And so the things we're doing now are quite involved, compared to what they were to start with."

Keeping it in the family, Sue's daughter and son-in-law Katy and Don Terlinden do the Hagen-Renaker order sheets twice a year, and Don does all the drawings. Originally Sue's brother David did the drawings.

Another interesting area of Sue's life is her musical side. The music is an enjoyable hobby, and a serious side line. Sue explains, "As you probably know, I have a bluegrass band which was the impulse behind 'Froggie Mountain Breakdown.' I also had a dear friend and musical mentor who played hammered dulcimer and hence I included that. I am very serious about it, and we (The Clay County Band) are busy recording our third CD. I was a folk-singer when I was in my teens and twenties and always incorporated that into my teaching. When I started working at Hagen-Renaker I gave that up and by 1980, I was not very happy about the lack of music in my life. I started going to a folk music club and that led to my joining a group of people who got together for bluegrass jams every Saturday night. I was in my first band by 1982, and had helped form a band in 1986. I formed Clay County in 1987, and we started doing recording projects. Most of my friends are musicians and most of my spare time is spent in social activities involving music. In addition, of course I spend time practicing and performing."

Portion of Froggie Mountain Breakdown band, with hammered dulcimer (2" tall), upright bass (3" tall), and fiddle (2.2" tall). The set also includes mandolin and banjo playing frogs and are currently available retail for $15 each.

Piano playing frog and grand piano. This piano also fits with other miniatures, including a polar bear and panda cubs. The frog measures 1" tall and has an approximate value of $5-7. The piano is 1.4" tall and came in black or white. The currently-made black one sells for $6 retail, and the white version has an approximate value of $12-15.

Members of The Clay County Band are Frank Abrahams on mandolin, Jim Dawson on banjo, Sue Nikas on guitar, and Jim Loque playing bass.

Sue goes on to explain, "My favorite part of Hagen-Renaker is developing new pieces. It is, of course, a team effort to work out the practical tasks of transforming the artist's sculpture into a piece that can be mass-produced. It is the most important and most creative part of the business and very satisfying to all of us."

Claire Weller comments that "Susan Renaker was my dearest friend all through school." Susan also has proven to be a friend to collectors and others. Under her control of the company, at least two special run pieces were issued for the Hagen-Renaker Collectors' Club. Also, according to Helen, Susan provides the musical specialty frogs that play the brass instruments to high school bands as prizes for marching band competitions. Then, at the suggestion of some music teachers, the company added the flute and clarinet. Yet another opportunity to combine the two important aspects of her life, pottery and music.

Susan Renaker seems to be a woman with many interests in her life, and the energy and opportunity to pursue them. The title of one of her CDs may well sum up Sue's life...it is titled "Satisfied Mind."

7

Mary Maxine Renaker

Mary Maxine Renaker is the fourth child of John and Maxine Renaker, born in 1951. As she recalls, "I grew up in Hagen-Renaker. I played in the factory after school when I was seven, dragging broken horses out of the finisher's trash cans and refinishing them with sponges and water. I loved to scour the sinks after the workers went home, and climb to the top of the bales of shredded newspaper in the packing dept. The workers were my friends."

"As for my work chronology at Hagen-Renaker, it began in a Quonset hut, when I was 14, after school decorating skunks for a couple of hours. Mother thought it would be good training for me, and it was. I traveled with my folks to the South Seas and Asia, then returned to work at 16, probably decorating again. I worked on and off in high school, 1965-1970, in the office, filing, after school. After high school I worked in the office again, from 1972-1974 I also worked in packing and the spray department...also glazing. I have fond memories of the older farm women who worked there. (I call them that because they were mainly from the midwest, and so strong, yet prim, and they wore aprons.) There were a couple of Mabels and a couple of Birdies, and one old farm woman that used to make us all laugh in glazing. There were jokes and good humor mostly all day in departments full of women, trading jokes and recipes...it was fun."

"I actually have more memories of individual workers in the factory, where I worked, than I do of the designers. I was too small to be invited into their 'workrooms' at the factory below Huntington Dr. in Monrovia, and that was the last time they had their own space in the factory. But I have fond memories of their visits, mostly because they were naturalists and showed me butterflies laying eggs on a fence, or their gardens and pets and ponds, which they all still have, by the way. Helen told me a wonderful story about living in Sierra Madre as a child and watching a cougar on the flagstones of their patio in the foothills, just napping and occasionally staring into her eyes with nothing between but a window screen. That's what makes her wonderful, and why she has had such a close rapport with my parents. They all love nature. (As do I.) Those people had fun, and it was their joy and creativity and that of both my parents that always made me love Hagen-Renaker and what made me most proud to be associated with them."

While attending Mt. San Antonio College and studying liberal arts, Mary met Eric Brazel, an art major. They married in 1974, and "Eric and I started Beachstone Beads in 1974. It was my dad's idea that we could make beads for the hanging planter trade and grind them in a tumbler to make them smooth like beachstones and therefore avoid having to finish or handle them much—save on labor costs so it could be cheap. Unfortunately, it was the tail end of the macramé bead, hanging planter biz, so I scampered out to the shed and found a bunch of old salt/pepper shaker molds from Walker Potteries, and had the idea of making necklaces of a Ma duck or chicken, and several baby ducks strung along with her on a rattail cord—just whimsical necklaces ala Parrot's Pearls. Then when I found an old Hagen-Renaker Teddy Bear, I thought why not make a hanging Christmas tree ornament? So we made the first 3-dimensional, ceramic Christmas tree ornament in the country in 1976." She

One of the "farm women" that Mary Renaker fondly remembers. This woman is working at the tedious task of cleaning seams and mold marks off the figurine.

also used a little Hagen-Renaker bird with wings spread, featured it in white with a 22 karat gold outline, and "they sold like crazy. We just called it the Dove."

The line expanded to include storybook characters, carousel animals, and more Christmas ornaments. "Our line was inspired by antique toys, antique children's books, carousel animals, and Mother Goose, and we didn't make miniatures. I didn't have designers, I thought up my line, and a 'copyist' put it in 3-D. My mom made Momcat with cake for me; I later added pie for the three little kittens. She also made Mr. & Mrs. Portleigh Pig and the toy elephant and the lamb with bonnet for our line."

Mary Renaker at Storybook Figurines booth.

Eric Brazel working in Storybook Figurines factory, putting liquid slip (clay) into molds.

Mom cat and kittens by Storybook Figurines. Mom measures 3.5" tall and the kittens are 1.75" tall. Approximate value for Mom cat $35-40 and for kittens $15-20.

Charming birthday party by Storybook Figurines. The large bear measure 3.25" and the little bear measures 1.5" tall. Approximate values range $15-40.

Storybook Figurine of carousel horse with gold foil oval sticker on belly. This colorful piece measures 3.5" tall and the approximate value is $25-30.

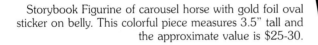

"When mom learned from Laurilyn Burson (designer Robyn Sikking's daughter) that Multifoods was seeking a buyer for their pottery division in San Marcos, she and dad decided to investigate. The Freeman-McFarlin Plant was literally in our own back yard, eleven miles east of our home and nursery in Encinitas. My parents installed Eric as plant manager, based on his work in our company, and me as national sales manager. All the pieces out of the San Marcos plant from 1980-May of '83, were under my husband's supervision. We later returned to our own company in Leucadia in May 1983 and produced Storybook Figurines and Ornaments until 1992."

Mary and Eric have one daughter. Alexis is "interactive editor" for a digital entertainment network in Santa Monica, California, and she hopes to be a producer some day. A really pretty, sweet girl, that Maxine Renaker says is "pretty on the inside, too."

When the pottery business began failing, Eric attended the San Francisco Culinary Academy. He gradu-ated in 1995 and currently works for Eos Restaurant and Wine Bar in San Francisco. He also works as a private chef. Mary is attending San Francisco State, working on a degree in conservation biology and library technology. She hopes to work in the library at the California Academy of Sciences, where she currently serves as a docent and a volunteer in the Biodiversity Resource Center Library there. As she explains, "I'm too old to go out in the field and be a conservation biologist myself, so I want to be able to help the younger generation find what they need to do research/ecological restoration and hook up with other preserve managers and people in the field working to preserve biodiversity all over the world."

It seems that the love of nature and animals that Mary developed in her early years through her parents and the designers at Hagen-Renaker may one day help to improve the environment for us all.

This head up pony was one of the pieces made at the Hagen-Renaker San Marcos factory under the direction of Eric Brazel. It stands 7" tall and was made in white and chestnut (color shown). It was designed by Maureen Love and the approximate value is $100-125.

The head down pony formed a set with the head up pony. It was designed by Maureen Love and is 5.5" tall. The pony came in both white (shown) and chestnut. Approximate value is $100-125.

The Designers' Workshop unicorn trio were formed from molds that were originally used for horses. This turning unicorn was originally the horse Sky Chief. Designed by Maureen Love, the flowers and horns were added in the mold shop, often by Rich Steckman. Standing at 5" tall, this unicorn has an approximate value of $85-95.

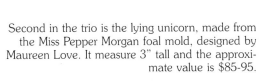

Second in the trio is the lying unicorn, made from the Miss Pepper Morgan foal mold, designed by Maureen Love. It measure 3" tall and the approximate value is $85-95.

The third unicorn is the head down version, made from the Mischief mold. It was designed by Maureen Love and measures 4" tall. The approximate value is $85-95.

8

Helen Perrin Farnlund

Somehow it seems appropriate that when you call Helen Perrin Farnlund and get her answering machine, the message says: "Hello...I'm out feeding the chickens, or I'm in the shower. Puss and Loki and Meringue don't write very well, so please leave a message." This fanciful message is very characteristic of the person who has been responsible for creating a large percentage of the adorable miniature animals done by Hagen-Renaker, as well as a few of the Designers' Workshop-sized critters (mama and baby zebra and giraffe sets). Laurilyn Burson describes Helen as whimsical..."She is as delightful as her work. She works very hard to get each of her pieces accurate as well as fanciful. When she does a mouse sculpture, for instance, she gets one from the pet store and keeps it by her, studying its movements as she works."

In Helen's own words,

Through high school and college (I went to Scripps) I was more interested in music, and I made things in my father's hobby shop. He liked making furniture, so he let me do that, too. After Scripps, I went to Art Center School in Los Angeles. I'd always liked to draw and I thought I might enjoy illustration, but I discovered oils and portrait painting. From Los Angeles, I went to Carmel to live and was fortunate enough to get a scholarship to the Carmel Art Institute where I studied under Armin Hansen and Paul Whitman, and learned a little sculpture and mold making from Finn Frolich. When my daughter was two I returned to southern California—the only time in my life I've been homesick was leaving Carmel; it is so beautiful and at that time there were only about 300 year-round inhabitants, lots of artists and writers, and tourists only in the summer. It is still beautiful but so big.

Faced with earning a living I went to work for Walker Pottery and learned to handle ceramic paints. It's not what I started out to do, but when you have to earn a living you do what you can. I had an opportunity to be a clerk at Hopkins, a friend of my mother's said it would be a good job, but I couldn't see myself as a clerk. I think she was kind of perturbed that I didn't take her up on it. Later I worked for Cleminson Pottery, painting and doing a few designs for them. John Renaker's mother worked at Walker's, and suggested me when John and Maxine were just starting their business and needed some decorating done—most fortunate for me!

As nearly as I can determine I started at H-R in 1946. The company grew so fast. We made dishes and shadowboxes at first, then I tried my hand at animals. I think the first was a clumsy hippo, and we went on from there and left the dishes behind. I was supposed to learn the ceramic business, from start to finish. But it grew so quickly, I ended up not doing much of anything but designing. It grew so quickly that I never got to do any of that other good stuff. I never did learn.

Maureen and I were the last designers to go, but I'm not sure of the date—1961 or 1962. Mr.

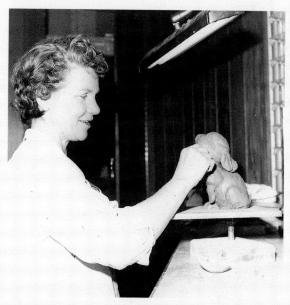

Helen Perrin (now Farnlund) working on a large rabbit figure in late 1959.

Farnlund and I moved to Santa Cruz in 1970. We taught music in the schools and privately and I did a very few models for H-R. Sometime in the late 70's or early 80's Maxine asked me to start designing again. I quit teaching in '86 to make more models. In 1990 we moved to Encinitas to be closer to work.

I've been so fortunate to be able to earn a living at something that is such fun to do. Not everybody gets that opportunity. It was great. My husband was in the same boat. He was a musician. We hear him in the old movies often. He also was an arranger in Hollywood. In the film 'Fantasia' there are a couple of shots of my husband in there. He was a percussionist, and in one shot the conductor is standing there and Emil's marimba was there and he's standing beside it. It's all in silhouette. If I didn't know who it was I wouldn't have guessed it was him. His name was Emil Farnlund. Emil was my music teacher when I was a girl. I love music. In high school I played percussion in orchestra and band. I've sold the drums and I sold all the marimbas except one. Emil died when he was 96. He lost his vision a few years before. He depended so much on his eyes for writing and arranging that he was very frustrated. I think that did him in.

These Fantasia unicorns must have special meaning to Helen, since her husband Emil Farnlund was in the Disney movie. The blue unicorn baby is 1.8" tall, the pale pink one also came in yellow and is 1.6" tall, and the adult blue unicorn is 2.75" tall. Approximate value of the small ones is $170-180 and the adult $190-200.

I used to go to the zoo in Griffin Park in Los Angeles before I made new models, and they had a wonderful old merry-go-round there. It's still there. So I would sketch there for a few hours, then before it was time to go home I'd have a merry-go-round ride. It was fun. I try not to be totally realistic. My designs are reasonably correct anatomically, but I take liberties to make them 'cutesy' and, hopefully appealing. A few of the first models were inspired by some of my child's story books, but mostly they were just little creatures made as round and cute as I could.

Live models are the best. Ducks, geese, chickens, rabbits and kittens grew up in my lap being models and, of course, became pets. One of the little rabbits loved running upstairs, into my daughter's room, out on the balcony, and jumping down into the bushes below. He'd do it 10 or 12 times before he had enough. There aren't very many pieces that I'm particularly proud of, though. I do like the badgers, otters, possums with babies on their back, and the small 'Puss in Boots.'

This miniature lop-eared rabbit sitting up on its hind legs has a partner that is crouching. Both are still currently made. This one is 1.8" tall and the retail price is $3.

This older rabbit duo was produced in the 60s. Mama rabbit is 1.5" tall and baby is 1" tall. Mama has an approximate value of $8-15 and baby $5-10, with the Aurasperse painted version being worth more.

The badger mama and her baby were produced in the 80s. She is .8" tall and her approximate value is $6-8.

Although not shown here, this opossum mama comes with a baby that hooks onto her tail with its tail, forming an adorable set. Mama stands .8" tall, was produced in the 80s, and has an approximate value of $7-9.

This Puss in Boots is very elaborate for a piece that is only 3.6" tall. Still currently produced, it was one of the first modern pieces made by Hagen-Renaker to utilize the iridescent colors that were used in the Little Horribles line years ago. Retail price is $25.

Over the years the designs became more elaborate as all our skills developed. To start with, we were only able to make 2-piece molds, so designs were limited. I've started putting several separate pieces to make a figure and stacking them up so that they can be cast in different colors, rather than being painted. Then they are assembled. The result is that you get better detail, because the opaque paint is rather thick and it destroys a lot of detail. So by casting it in the proper slip color, I don't have to paint it and it comes out a lot better. Sue is asking Maureen to do that sort of thing now, and Maureen hates me for it! It's harder to do. Now we make multiple piece molds, and add on units to the figures; 'Puss in Boots' is five units glued together.

Some before firing, some after. The mini music frogs all have arms added before firing and instruments glued on after. I think the added detail certainly adds to the appeal.

My jaw drops every time something like this comes up, because we started this just to earn a living, and I just felt very blessed to be able to earn a living at something that I enjoyed doing. I started out as a portrait painter. My jaw just drops every time I realize the interest that people are showing in what we were doing, and how they buy these little things by the jillions. I just can't imagine. I had a young woman write to me from Puerto Rico wanting an autograph.

I have one daughter, and she has two kids. And I do have chickens!

The white squatty hen was made in the 50s and has an attached chick. The brown hen was made much later and the chick came unattached. Both are 1" tall and have an approximate value of $12-15.

It is easy to think that these comical draft horses were part of the series produced by Tom Masterson, but they were actually designed by Helen Farnlund. They stand 3.25" tall, were made in the late 40s to early 50s, and have an approximate value of $25-30.

This whimsical set of turtles was produced in the late 40s. Both sizes were made in blue and in pink with various decorations. Mama turtle is 2" tall and her baby is 1.25" tall. Approximate values are $12-15 for mama and $6-8 for baby.

The lying calf was produced with a cow in the late 40s and early 50s. It measures 1.25 tall and has an approximate value of $8-10.

This trio was made in both brown (shown) and in a soft gray. Waking fawn measures 1.5" tall, standing fawn is 2.6" tall, and the sleeping fawn is .6" tall. All have an approximate value of $8-10.

Another good example of the facial detail of the early days, this baby squirrel was produced in the early 50s. It measures 1" tall and has an approximate value of $6-8.

This is an early version of the mouse mama. It has a black tail, nails, and other details. The mold is still in current use, but without all the elaborate decorating. She stands 1" tall and this version has an approximate value of $8-10. The current one with gray tail retails for $2.

Known as either Bear Ma or Bear Pa by Hagen-Renaker, this grumpy bear stands 2.5" tall and has an approximate value of $8-10.

Looking rather smug, these fez-wearing camels were made in the 50s and 60s. Camel mama is 1.6" tall and her baby is .8" tall. Approximate value for the mama is $20-25 and for the baby $15-20. The mama without fez currently sells for $5 retail.

Queenie the Cocker Spaniel was produced in the mid-50s, one of the few Pedigree Dogs not designed by Tom Masterson. She stands 4.75" tall and has an approximate value of $100-120.

Dash is madly dashing after his tail. One of Queenie's puppies, he measures 2.5" tall and has an approximate value of $60-65.

Dot rounds out the family of three, at a height of 3". Her approximate value is $60-65.

Molly rabbit shows a very clear example of the Hagen-Renaker name sticker used on the Designers' Workshop animals. It has the animal's name, the year produced, and the Designers' Workshop name. Molly measures 4" tall and came in both brown (almost gray, the color shown) and in white. Older versions of Molly have an approximate value of $45-50, the ones reissued in the 80s have an approximate value of $25-30.

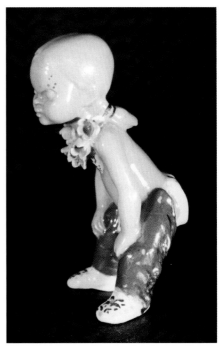

This little Indian was designed by Helen Perrin Farnlund but was never produced by Hagen-Renaker.

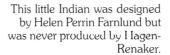

Figaro is the adorable kitten from the Disney movie *Pinocchio*. Note the special Walt Disney/Figaro/Hagen-Renaker sticker on his tummy. He stands 2.25" tall and has an approximate value of $140-160.

Sassy the reaching tabby kitten was produced in the mid-60s. The same mold was produced in Siamese cat color and called Quan Yen. Measuring 3.75" tall, Sassy has an approximate value of $45-50. Quan Yen has an approximate value of $35-40.

Snowflake the fawn is part of a large family of three fawns, a buck, and a doe. Originally produced in the 50s, the family was reissued in the 80s. The elaborate facial detail of this fawn dates it to the earlier run. It stands 3.25" tall and has an approximate value of $35-40. More recent ones have a slightly lower value of approximately $25-30.

Raindrop the fawn was also produced in the 50s, and sports the Hagen-Renaker sticker showing its name, date and the words Designers' Workshop. Standing 2.5" tall, the older versions of this fawn have an approximate value of $35-40 and the more recent ones are approximately $25-30.

Twinkle is an example of more recent production techniques. The facial detail is much simpler. Standing 3.5" tall, this fawn's approximate value is $25-30. One produced in the 50s would have an approximate value of $35-40.

Sentinel the buck was also produced in two versions. This example from the 80s was designed by Helen Perrin Farnlund and stands 8" tall. The 50s version was designed by Tom Masterson and was only 6.75" tall. The approximate value for this version of Sentinel is $100-125.

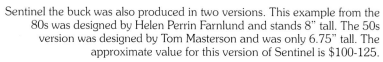

Heidi's Goat was produced in the 80s with the added flowers and bell. Prior to this, the mold was released in the 50s and 60s as Gretchen and came in brown without all the extra trim. Standing 4.5" tall, Heidi's Goat has an approximate value of $45-50. Gretchen in brown has an approximate value of $70-75.

Heidi is the brown goat Gretchen's kid. Produced only in the mid-50s, Heidi measures 2.5" tall and has an approximate value of $80-85. She also has a 3" standing brother Peterli (not shown).

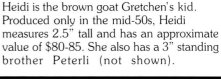

These awesome giraffes are some of the largest pieces made in the 50s. The giraffe mama stands 8.5" tall and her baby is 5" tall. The elaborate decorating is very characteristic of that period. Approximate value for the mama is $150-160 and for the baby $80-100.

Papa, baby, and mama chipmunk do not have names, which was unusual for early 50s Designers' Workshop pieces. Papa measures 1.8" tall, baby is 1.75" tall, and mama with the acorn is 2.75" tall. The approximate value for the adults is $40-45 and for the baby is $25-30.

Mother Goose was produced in the 80s. Note the real lace inside of her bonnet. She stands 6.5" tall and has an approximate value of $70-80.

Little boy gosling and little girl gosling were produced along with Mother Goose in the mid-80s. The boy gosling is 3.25" tall and the girl is 3" tall. Their approximate value is $25-30 each.

Puss in Boots was originally produced for the Designers' Workshop in the mid-80s before being released in the smaller, specialty size. This one has real lace trim around the sleeves. Standing at 6.5" tall, his approximate value is $100-110.

The Little Red Hen is another Designers' Workshop piece from the mid-80s that later came out in the specialty scale. She measures 6.5" tall and has an approximate value of $100-125.

This delightful grouping of water dwellers belongs to Helen Perrin Farnlund, so their decoration is more elaborate then the production run pieces. The box turtle mama is .625" tall, the box turtle baby is .5" tall, and the frog is .625" tall. The lily pad measures 1.6" across. They have all been produced for many years, so their prices will vary depending on the intricacy of their decorating. Approximate values range from $2-16.

Professor Owl, the baby barn owl, and the book were also production pieces, but these particular ones are uniquely decorated since they are Helen's. Professor Owl stands 1.1" tall, the baby owl is .625" tall, and the book is .25" tall. Approximate values for the factory pieces are $12-15 for the professor, $4-5 for the baby, and $18-20 for the book.

Papa cat looks handsome in this coat color, but was never available commercially this way. He did come in gray or black and white, and the stalking kitten came in gray. Papa is 2.25" tall and the kitten is 1.5" tall. The milk bottle stands 1.25" tall. Approximate value on Papa cat is $3-15, the kitten is $6-8, and the milk bottle is $12-15.

Mama and baby parrot sport very colorful feathers, much more elaborate than the production run versions. It is a real treat to view these custom critters. The parrot mama stands 1.25" tall and her baby is .75" tall. The factory decorated mama and baby were both available in glaze and Aurasperse versions. Parrot mama has an approximate value of $10-18 and baby of $7-10, with the Aurasperse ones being more valuable.

Miniature hound dawgs came in a variety of colors, including brown, yellow, or gray with darker ears. The large dawg is 1.4" tall and the playing puppy is .4" tall. The hydrant is approximately 1.25" tall, but came in two sizes. Red is a hard color to achieve in glaze, so this red was painted on, but is now wearing off. Approximate values are $5-10 for the adult dawg, $5-7 for the puppy, and $5-7 for the hydrant.

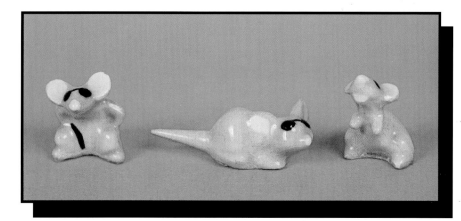

The Three Blind Mice. They stand about .625" tall and have an approximate value of $8-10 each.

Officially known as pixies, these adorable folks are also referred to by collectors as Petal People to differentiate them from the Millesan Drews pixies. The throwing pixie stands 2.5" tall, the seated one (should be on a snail) is 2.4" tall, the pixie with hand outstretched (should have a stick) is 2.75" tall and the girl is 2.75" tall. Made in the early 50s, all have an approximate value of $40-50.

This miniature giraffe family was only made in the early 50s. Mama giraffe stands 3" tall, and both babies are 1" tall. Approximate value for the mama is $35-40 and $15-18 for each baby.

These two graceful young ballerinas are part of a set that was made in the late 50s. The missing member is balancing on one foot, with the other stretched out behind her. These two stand 2.75" tall and have an approximate value of $40-50.

This cartoony cattle duo has been made in a creamy white, reddish brown, light and dark brown, and this striking color of black and white with gold horns and hooves. The bull is 2" tall and the cow is 1.5" tall. Approximate values range from $12-20, with this color being the most valuable.

Indian elephant mama and baby were produced in the early 60s. Mama stands 2.5" tall and baby 1.25" tall. Approximate values are $30-35 for the mama and $5-9 for baby.

The seated puppy is 1" tall and was only made in the early 60s. The adult has been issued in this color and also as a Dalmatian. She is 2" tall. In this color she has an approximate value of $18-20, but as a Dalmatian only $4-5 as it is a more recent color. The puppy has an approximate value of $12-14.

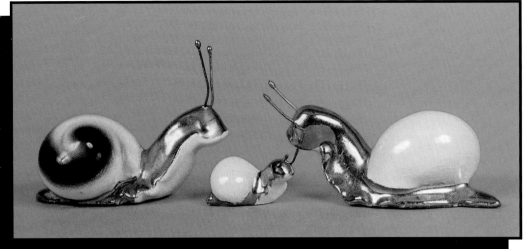

Escargot Maman and her escargot bébé are very striking in this color combination. There are two versions of Maman shown here, with the more recent one having the gray swirl on her shell. Maman is .9" tall and her bébé is .4" tall. Approximate values are $8-12 for each.

Standing donkey mama and baby were made for several years from the 60s to the 80s. Mama stands 2" tall and baby is 1.5" tall. The approximate value for mama is $10-20 and for baby $5-10, with the matte versions being more valuable than the glossy versions.

This standing pig measures 1.1" tall and has been in production since the mid-80s. The current retail price is $3.

The black-footed ferret was only made a short time in the early 90s. He stands 1" tall and has an approximate value of $8-10.

This beaver is a good example of how Helen was able to make her animals anatomically correct, yet cute. His paws are up because he should be gnawing on a stump which is not shown. The beaver stands 1" tall and has an approximate value of $4-5 for the more recent reddish-brown version (color shown) to $10-12 for the Aurasperse version.

Cat and fiddle were designed to go with the Mouse Band on page 159. He stands 2.8" tall and has an approximate value of $15-18.

The sea horse was molded as a separate piece from the base, then they were glued together. Note that the orange one faces a different direction than the blue and green ones. They stand 2.5" tall and have an approximate value of $20-22.

These three Disney critters were all designed by Helen in the mid-50s. Chip, the chipmunk with the acorn, and his pal Dale both measure 1.25" tall and have approximate values of $65-80 each. Bambi the fawn was produced both with and without the butterfly on his tail. He measures 1.6" tall, was produced in the late 50s, and has an approximate value of $130-150, with the butterfly version being more valuable.

9

Maureen Love

"My God, what a fabulous, talented person she is; and devoted to her work! She lives for the horses; all animals for that matter. Just delightful!" This quote is from Martha Armstrong Hand, when asked what she remembered about Maureen Love. It seems to pretty well sum up everyone's feelings about Maureen. Helen Perrin Farnlund further explains, "Everything Maureen does is very realistic. And she does such a good job. She's such a neat gal. She's different than most people. She's very, very honest in her whole attitude, personality, and relations with people. She's not a phony person."

Maureen went to work at Hagen-Renaker as a decorator in 1951. Prior to that, she had several varied experiences, including, according to Jim Renaker, "She was a welder during the 2nd World War. Worked at Kaiser Shipyard, building Liberty Ships. They hired lots of young girls in those days because they could get into places within the hull of the ship and weld where a man couldn' t get his shoulders in. They used them for the tight work and the hard places. She came into the kiln room at Hagen-Renaker one time and found me doing a little welding job, and asked me if she could try it. She surprised me. She took the rod and the rod stuck. She says ' Give me a bigger rod, and more heat.' With all the heat I could put out of that machine, and a 1/4" diameter rod she could weld pretty well. It was a big surprise."

Maureen attended the California School of Fine Arts in San Francisco to receive her early art training. She then worked for a time drawing pastel portraits of horses for people. Prior to working for Hagen-Renaker, she recalls doing some work for Twin Wintons Pottery, making larger, rather than miniature, pieces. She also worked on her own at home, with her own kiln and molds, so she had an understanding of the process.

Once she was hired by Hagen-Renaker, she worked as a decorator for quite a while. How the transition to designer exactly occurred is lost in time, but either Maureen brought in some of her original work from home for John Renaker to see, or Nell Bortells saw her work and lobbied John to get her into the design department, but the result was that no other designer wanted to make horses from that point on.

Maureen Love in late 1959.

Understanding the animal that she sculpts is very important to Maureen. She accomplishes this by making numerous sketches. In her own words, "I like to draw, and I did do lots of life sketches. I did it primarily for a purpose, though, because if I was going to make a model of an animal then I would sketch it first. I think that you can get a better idea of the form and conformation. Rather than purely just going out and taking pictures, if you go out, it takes a whole lot longer to sketch. But if you sketch it that's a lot different; you learn a lot more."

One of the places she frequently visited was the Wagon Wheel Ranch, owned by friends Jimmie & Edna Nelson. Many of her beautiful Arabian sculptures, both for Hagen-Renaker and her originals, came from horses at that ranch. She also spent some time at the OK Ranch, drawing Appaloosas. Maggie (O'Shea) Kennedy, co-owner of the ranch, recalls chatting with Maureen while she was there to sketch her horses and being told that Maureen "likes to go personally to the place where the animals are that she is sculpting."

With her deep love of horses, one might wonder if she was ever a rider. Her reply is "Very, very little. When I was a kid actually, I had a friend who was the substitute school teacher. She had two horses, and I used to go riding with her sometimes. But this was very limited, and I wasn't much of a rider. I liked it, of course, because I liked the horses, but it was just for fun."

In 1962 Maureen was released from Hagen-Renaker, one of the last designers to go. She worked free-lance for that period of time, with a few other California pottery companies, with McAfee's, and on her own. In 1968 she married P.G. Calvert, who she met at Santa Anita race track while sketching horses there. P.G. printed the tip sheet, and he was timing the horses when they ran into each other. She had an immediate family of four children as a result of that marriage. Sadly, a little over a year later P.G. died of lung cancer.

In 1980 Hagen-Renaker was able to once again hire her back full-time, but this time she made arrangements to do her sculpting work at home. She draws great inspiration from her surroundings; her yard and garden are brimming with animal and plant life. Also, she explains, "I can walk down to the ocean. I can't see it from my house, but it's nice. I live near Moonlight Beach. I get up around 4 am. It takes me a little while to get going, but I do better in the morning, as far as being creative. When the weather's nice, I do quite a bit on my models outside. I like it outside."

Maureen also has very strong opinions on how sculptures should look, since she favors the natural appearance. For example, when asked about glossy finish as opposed to matte, her response is "I think the majority of the people prefer the shiny glaze. I don't!! It reflects all the light so much, you can't see the sculpture nearly as well on a shiny piece. The detail and muscles. Let's face it...unless it's something that just fell in a pond and climbed out, why, nothing's shiny like that. Not that shiny!"

Nell Bortells mentioned that Maureen does not like the tri-color eye, either. When questioned further on this, Maureen's reply is "One reason I didn't like the tri-color too well was because a lot of the decorators didn't know how to do it. So it was better to have just one dark color

to worry about then it was to have two colors and the white. When I decorate a horse I always use just the black and the white. To my mind it's too small of a model to make all those colors in the eye. I think it's more effective without it. When you look at a horse, without going up and studying him really close, your general impression is just a big, dark eye. Of course, if I did a painting, then I would make the eye like that, but that would be like a head study or something like that that was larger, you see. Probably about life-size in fact."

Laurilyn Burson is one of Maureen's greatest fans. She says Maureen "is one of the most authentic persons I ever met—takes life as it comes doing her very best! She takes a 90 year old lady shopping every week and the lady has no clue to her talent or fame. I feel that Maureen is a national treasure! She is so talented and such a unique person! I used to watch Charles Kuralt and in one of his programs he mentioned that no one 'made things' any more—I wanted to write and tell him about Maureen, but she declined."

Maureen and Laurilyn have joined efforts in a company called "Made With Love," and they produce 6" scale horses that Maureen sculpts and Laurilyn decorates. They may also produce some of Maureen's famous birds, which Laurilyn describes as being "so realistic you expect them to move." It is wonderful to have yet another outlet for enjoying the work of Maureen Love!

Clydesdale stallion, available in this rough finish or in a glossy glazed finish from Made With Love. He stands 5.75" tall and the retail price for this horse is $150.

Arabian horse Abu Farwa with the tricolored eyes on the left and the black dot eyes on the right.

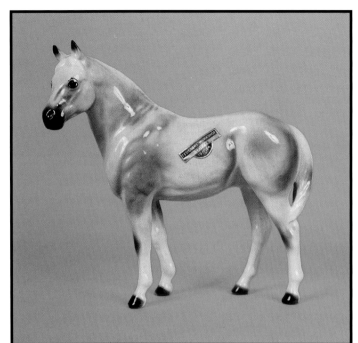

Topper the Quarter Horse stallion was only produced in the mid-50s and only in this glossy palomino color, although the shade varied from light to dark. He stands 5.75" tall and has an approximate value of $275-300.

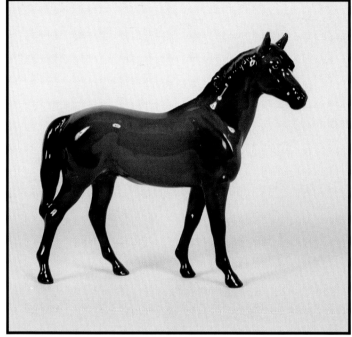

Payday the Thoroughbred stallion was only produced in the mid-50s, and only in this glossy bay color. He stands 6.25" tall and has an approximate value of $275-300.

Abdullah the Arabian stallion came in two versions. The one on the left was produced in the 50s, stood 6.25" tall, and only came in white. The one on the right was the revised model, produced in the 60s and standing only 6" tall. The right one came in both white (shown) and chestnut. The approximate value for each is $375-400.

Mischief is part of the trio of yearlings produced in the late 50s. He came in both palomino and white (shown) and stands 4" tall. His approximate value is $275-300.

Sky Chief is also part of the yearling trio, produced in the late 50s and late 60s. He came in palomino (shown), white, and buckskin. He is 4.75" tall and has an approximate value of $275-300.

Drum Major rounds out the trio of yearlings, produced in the late 50s and late 60s. He came in buckskin, palomino, and white (shown). He is 5.25" tall and has an approximate value of $275-300.

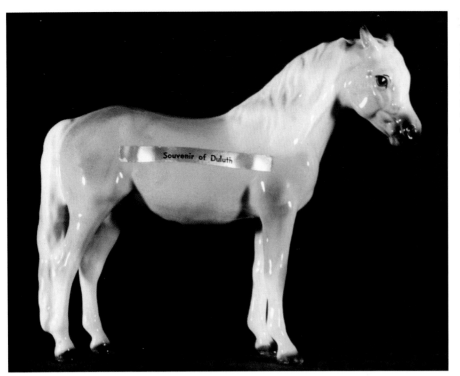

Heather the Morgan mare came in white, palomino (shown), and a variety of shades of brown. Note the "Souvenir of Duluth" sticker on her side. Many shops would add their own stickers to Hagen-Renakers. She stands 5" tall, was only produced in the mid-50s, and has an approximate value of $375-400.

Thunder the Morgan stallion was produced in the mid-50s and stands 5.5" tall. He came in white, palomino (shown), and various shades of brown. His approximate value is $275-300.

Peggy Lou the bucking Morgan foal is quite the unusual piece, as she balances on her two front hooves and her nose. She came in chestnut (shown) and palomino, and was only issued in 1959, possibly due to high breakage rates. She is 4" tall and has an approximate value of $375-400.

Scamper the grazing Morgan foal illustrates the lovely brown color that was also found on the adult Morgans Heather and Thunder. Scamper also came in white and palomino, was produced in the mid-50s, and stands 3" tall. There were many excellent copies of this horse produced overseas. Approximate value $140-160.

Clover the lying Morgan foal rounds out this Morgan family. She was produced in the mid-50s in white (shown), palomino, and brown. This mold was another one that was frequently copied overseas. She measures 2.5" tall and has an approximate value of $140-150.

Roan Lady the Tennessee Walking Horse was made intermittently from the 50s through the 70s. She came in white, gray, and this color which some consider a variant on gray called doeskin. She stands 7.25" tall and has an approximate value of $450-500.

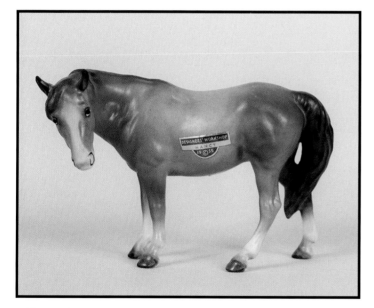

Nancy the mare was produced intermittently through the 50s and 60s. The shading on her may vary from browns to rose-colored. She stands 3.75" tall and has an approximate value of $325-350.

Tony is the newborn foal of Nancy. This fragile little fellow measures 3.25" tall and has an approximate value of $175-200.

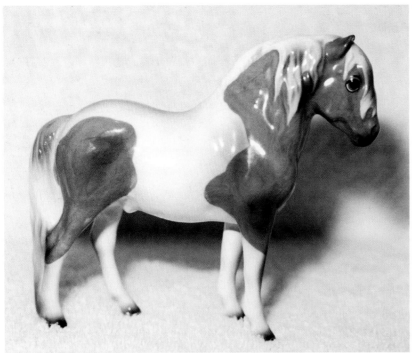

Wrangler the Shetland Pony stallion stands 4" tall. He was produced in chestnut, gray pinto(shown), red dun, brown, and brown pinto. His approximate value is $275-300.

Maydee the Shetland Pony mare was produced in brown pinto, gray pinto, red dun, brown, and chestnut (shown). She stands 3.5" tall and has an approximate value of $250-300.

Rascal the Shetland Pony foal completes the family. All three pieces were made intermittently during the 50s and 60s. Rascal also came in brown pinto (two shades are shown), gray pinto, red dun, brown, and chestnut. He stands 2.75" tall and has an approximate value of $175-200.

Fez the rearing Arabian stallion came in two sizes. The 8.5" version on the left was made in the mid-50s and came in white or gray (shown). The 7.75" version on the right was made in the late 60s and also came in white or gray (shown). The approximate value for each is $375-400.

The turning Arabian might more appropriately be called the prancing Arabian, but Hagen-Renaker gave him the name turning Arabian. He stands 6" tall, was produced in the late 60s, and came in white or chestnut (shown). His approximate value is $375-400.

Zara the 6.5" Arabian mare shares a name with a larger model. She was made from the late 50s to the mid-70s in white and various shades of gray. Here she is shown in white on the left and doeskin gray on the right. She is also found in a much darker gray. Approximate value $125-175.

Amir the Arabian stallion measures 6" tall. He was produced in white (right) and doeskin (left), plus other shades of gray. Produced from the late 50s to the mid-70s he has an approximate value of $125-175.

Zilla the standing Arabian foal was produced in white (shown) and various shades of gray, including doeskin, from the late 50s to the mid-70s. She also shares her name with a larger horse. She measures 5" tall and has an approximate value of $80-100.

Fez the lying Arabian foal rounds out this Arabian family. He measures 2.75" tall and was produced from the late 50s until the early 70s. He came in white (shown) and various shades of gray. His approximate value is $100-125.

Sheba the Arabian mare is 7" tall and was produced intermittently throughout the 50s, 60s and 70s. She came in white (shown), and various shades of gray. Her approximate value is $325-375.

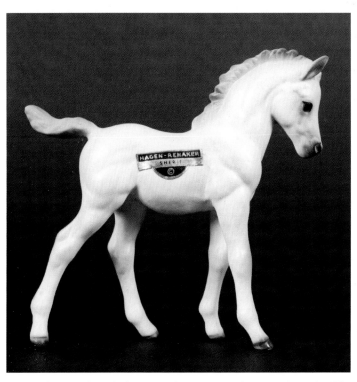

Sherif the Arabian foal was made intermittently throughout the 50s and 60s. It came in white (shown) and gray (considered rare). The height is 4.25" and approximate value is $150-200.

Ferseyn the Arabian stallion rounds out this family grouping. He stands 7.75" tall and comes in steel gray (shown), doeskin, and white. His approximate value is $325-375.

Crusader the Percheron was only produced in matte white, and measures 6.25" tall. It was made in the late 50s and mid-60s, and has an approximate value of $700-750.

Bedouin horse and rider is one of only three Designers' Workshop horses with a rider made by Hagen-Renaker. This piece was made in the late 50s and measures 9.5" tall. Approximate value is $900-1000.

Honora, the large America Saddlebred Horse, measures 8" tall and came in white or brown(shown). It was only produced a short time from the late 50s to early 60s, and has an approximate value of $375-400.

This smaller American Saddlebred Horse is sometimes also called Honora. It came in brown (shown), white, and a special limited run of palomino. It was produced intermittently in the 60s and 80s, measures 6.75" tall, and has an approximate value of $150-175.

Lipizzaner stallion is another horse in the Designers' Workshop line that does not have a name. It was made intermittently from the late 50s until the mid-80s, with some of the older ones mounted on wooden bases. Most were on ceramic bases, as shown here. He measures 6.5" tall and has an approximate value of $175-250, depending on age.

Brookside Stella the Hackney Pony was mounted on a wooden base in the 50s and on this ceramic base in the 80s. She came in dark bay and buckskin (color shown), and stands 5.5" tall. Approximate value for older ones is $400-450 and $250-275 for more recent ones.

Zara the large Arabian mare measures 9" tall and was produced in white, gray (color shown), palomino, and brown. Her years of production range widely from the mid-50s to the mid-80s, so her approximate value is hard to determine, as older pieces are worth $350-400 while the more recent releases are only worth $175-200.

Amir the large Arabian stallion measures 9" tall. He was produced in white, palomino, brown, and gray (color shown). Made intermittently from the mid-50s until the mid-80s, the older pieces have an approximate value of $350-400 and the more recent ones are worth $175-200.

Zilla the large Arabian foal measures 7" tall and was produced in palomino, white, brown, and gray (shown). Made intermittently from the mid-50s until the mid-80s, the older ones have an approximate value of $175-200 while the more recent ones are worth $80-100.

Lippet the Morgan stallion stands 6.25" tall. He was made in chestnut (color shown), palomino, and dark bay. His production started in the late 50s and ended in the 80s, and his approximate values range from $100-175 depending on age.

Forever Amber is the Morgan mare that goes with Lippet. She is 5" tall and also came in chestnut (shown), bay, and palomino. She was produced from the late 50s intermittently until the mid-80s, and her approximate value is $100-120.

Miss Pepper the lying Morgan foal came in chestnut and palomino (shown). She was only produced from the late 50s until the early 70s, and has an approximate value of $90-100.

Roughneck is the standing Morgan foal that goes with this family. He was made in palomino, chestnut (shown), dark bay, and white (only in the late 50s). He stands 4.5" tall and was produced from the late 50s intermittently until the mid-80s. His approximate value is $50-90, with the white version worth approximately $125-150.

Erin the Quarter Horse mare was produced in the early 60s and again in the mid-80s. The earlier version was buckskin (color shown) and the later version was dark bay. There was also a special run done in palomino in the 80s. She stands 6" tall and has an approximate value of $125-200, with the older ones being worth more.

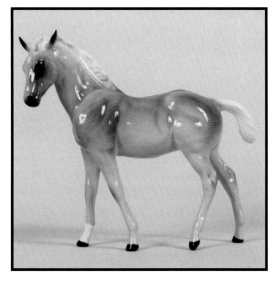

Shamrock is the Quarter Horse foal that goes with Erin. It is shown here in the special run palomino color. It also came in buckskin and dark bay. It was made from the early 60s until the early 70s, then again in the 80s. It stands 5" tall and has an approximate value of $75-125, with the earlier buckskin being the more valuable color.

Daisy the Mustang mare was produced in bay, buckskin (color shown), red/brown pinto, and white (considered rare). She was made throughout the 60s, and stands 5.5" tall. Her approximate value is $275-300.

Comanche the Mustang stallion came in buckskin, dark brown, and red-brown. He stands 6.25" tall, was produced throughout the 60s, and has an approximate value of $300-350, with the buckskin color being the most valuable.

Butch the Mustang foal was produced throughout the 60s and stands 4.5" tall. He was made in bay, buckskin, and a red-brown pinto (color shown), although the only white markings are one high stocking and a white face. Approximate value $160-175.

Maverick the Quarter Horse stallion was produced in the late 50s and again in the late 60s. He only came in this buckskin color, but this particular one is a factory error, as he usually has black stockings on his legs. He measures 6" tall and has an approximate value of $450-500.

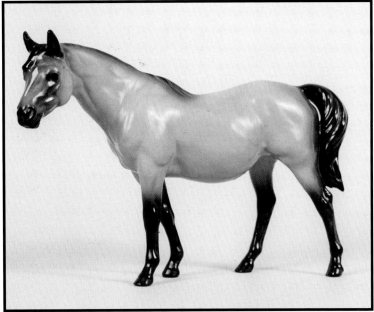

Comella the Thoroughbred mare came in this lovely buckskin color, and also in dark bay. She was produced in the 60s and early 70s, and stands 5.5" tall. Her approximate value is $300-325.

Vanguard the Thoroughbred foal matches his mare in buckskin and dark bay. He was produced in the 60s and early 70s, and stands 4.75" tall. He has an approximate value of $200-225.

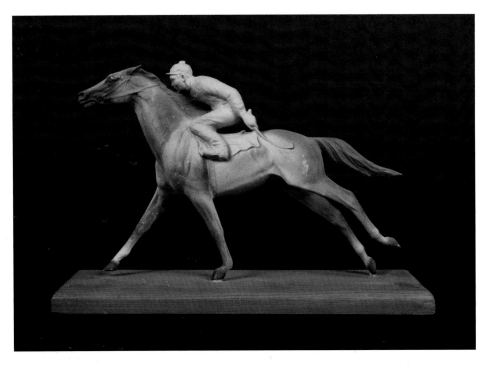

The Thoroughbred and jockey stand 6.5" tall, and has been seen decorated with colors on the jockey's silks, the saddle blanket, and the horse. This example is either unfinished or unfired, and is mounted on a base that is not original. The model was only made a short time in the early 60s and is considered very rare. There is now a Thoroughbred horse and jockey in the specialty line that closely resembles this piece.

Sun Cortez the turning Mustang was made intermittently throughout the 50s, 60s, and 80s. He was produced in palomino, chestnut, gray, white, and black (color shown). He stands 6" tall and has an approximate value of $175-225.

King Cortez the rearing Mustang is part of a set of three Mustang stallions. He was made intermittently throughout the 50s, 60s, and 80s and measures 8" tall. He has been produced in white, gray, chestnut, black, and palomino (color shown). His approximate value is $200-250.

Don Cortez the head up Mustang stands 6.5" tall and was made intermittently throughout the 50s, 60s, and 80s. He stands 6.5" tall and came in chestnut, gray, palomino, black, and white (color shown). His approximate value is $175-225.

Nataf the Arabian stallion and the Quarter Horse stallion collectors refer to as Metalchex are the largest horses that have been in regular production at Hagen-Renaker. Both horses were only produced in the 80s at the San Marcos facility. Nataf stands 12" tall and was only made in white. The Quarter Horse stallion is 11.75" tall and came in buckskin (shown) and chestnut. Both of these massive horses have an approximate value of $275-350.

This mule was only made in the mid-80s at the San Marcos factory. It stands 8" tall and came only in this color, but in either a matte or glossy finish. The approximate value for this mule is $200-225.

Produced in the 80s, this Quarter Horse mare represents the change in the breed standard compared to the older Quarter Horse Two Bits that Hagen-Renaker produced 25 years earlier. She stands 8" tall and was available in bay, gray, or chestnut (color shown) plus a special run in bay Appaloosa. Her approximate value is $175-225, with the Appaloosa being the most valuable.

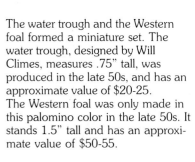

The anvil and the Percheron were a miniature set. The anvil was designed by Will Climes in the late 50s, and measures 1.4" tall. It has an approximate value of $40-50.

This hitching post was produced in the late 50s and formed a set with the miniature Morgan mare. The hitching post is 1.75" tall, was designed by Will Climes, and has an approximate value of $40-50.

The water trough and the Western foal formed a miniature set. The water trough, designed by Will Climes, measures .75" tall, was produced in the late 50s, and has an approximate value of $20-25.
The Western foal was only made in this palomino color in the late 50s. It stands 1.5" tall and has an approximate value of $50-55.

Sea Biscuit the Thoroughbred race horse came with this racing ticket in the 60s. He is 2.75" tall and was made intermittently in the 60s in bay and buckskin and in the 90s in chestnut. The horse is now mounted on a ceramic base, and is currently available at a retail price of $9, but the older versions have an approximate value of $70-75.

Native Dancer the Thoroughbred race horse was only made in the mid-60s. He was produced in this steel gray color, and measures 3" tall. His approximate value is $70-75.

This prancing Arabian stallion and Arabian foal were produced intermittently throughout the 50s, 60s, and 70s. They came in white (shown), doeskin gray, and bay. The stallion stands 3.25" tall and the foal is 2" tall. The foal also came in a slight variation with the tail pointed up. Approximate values are $70-100 for the stallion and $30-40 for the foal, with the bay color being the most valuable.

The standing Arabian mare and stallion were produced in white (shown) and doeskin gray intermittently throughout the 50s, 60s, and 70s. The mare stands 2.5" tall and the stallion is 3" tall. Their approximate values are $50-65 each.

Known only as the head down horse, this charmer came in black pinto, buckskin, palomino, and Appaloosa (shown). It measures 2.25" tall and was produced in the 60s. It has an approximate value of $85-125, with the black pinto being the most valuable color.

Miniature rearing stallion came in palomino (shown) and in brown. It was produced in the 60s and early 70s, stands 3.5" tall, and has an approximate value of $70-75.

The companion piece, the head up horse, also came in black pinto, buckskin, palomino, and Appaloosa (shown). It measures 3" tall and was produced throughout the 60s and early 70s. It has an approximate value of $75-125, with the black pinto being the most valuable color.

The Percheron draft horse was produced in the 50s and 60s in this white color. It stands 2.75" tall and has an approximate value of $70-80. The version with the harness came in white or chestnut. The white has an approximate value of $75-80 and the chestnut, which was produced much later, has an approximate value of $20-25.

Miniature Morgan family consisting of stallion, standing foal, and mare. The stallion is 2.75" tall, the foal 2" tall, and the mare 3" tall. The set came in chestnut (shown) and palomino and were produced from the late 50s until the early 70s. The approximate values are $55-65 stallion, $30-35 foal, and $60-70 mare.

Thoroughbred mare and foal were made in the 60s and 70s in buckskin (shown) and bay. The mare stands 3" tall and the foal is 2" tall. Their approximate values are $60-65 for the mare and $30-35 for the foal. The foal was later reissued without the mare in the 80s in black and has an approximate value of $18-20.

Head down pony was issued with and without a harness. It stands 2.25" tall. The chestnut version and the circus pony with the plume were produced in the 50s and have an approximate value of $70-75. The version without the plume was made in the 80s, came in a blue or yellow harness and has an approximate value of $20-25.

Head up pony was issued with and without a harness. It stands 2.4" tall. The chestnut version and the circus pony with the plume were produced in the 50s and have an approximate value of $70-75. The version without the plume (not shown) was made in the 80s, came in a green, lavender, maroon, or pink harness, and has an approximate value of $20-25.

Measuring only 1.25" tall for the adults and 1" for the foals, this series of horses known as the mini mini horses are the smallest made by Hagen-Renaker. The mares are the prancing ones and the stallions are the standing ones. A variety of colors were available, including various shades of buckskin, brown, palomino, and white. Made in the 50s, 60s, 70s, and 90s, their values vary with the adults worth approximately $8-20 and foals $3-12. The glossy palomino and buckskin colors are the most common and least valuable.

Tom the walking cat was produced in the 50s and 60s in gray (shown) and orange tabby. He stands 5" tall and has an approximate value of $70-75.

Sugar the standing kitten is part of Tom's family. She stands 2.25" tall and came in this striped color, gray, and orange tabby. Produced in the 50s and 60s, she has an approximate value of $40-45.

Grizzly Bear had no other name. He stands 7.75" tall on his rock slab and was made intermittently in the 60s, 70s, and 80s. The oldest color is brown, then later he was released in white and in gold. His approximate value is $125-175.

Toulouse goose was made for a very brief period in the mid-50s. He stands 7" tall and has an approximate value of $140-150.

Mallard drake and Mallard hen were produced in the 60s in these stunning colors, and the hen returned in the 80s in white. The drake stands 5.5" tall and the hen 2.75" tall. The approximate values are $70-75 each for the older ducks, and $35-40 for the hen in white.

Daniel the large frog is the largest of three Designers' Workshop frogs designed by Maureen Love. He measures 2.6" tall and was produced intermittently during the 50s, 60s, and 70s. His approximate value is $30-35.

Resting pheasant was only produced in the mid-80s. It is 4" tall and 13" long. The approximate value is $45-50.

Ching Wu (left) and Ah Choo (right) were produced intermittently throughout the 50s and 60s. This Siamese coloring sometimes had these slit pupils, but usually the pupils were more round and full. These two cats also came in Abyssinian and blue point, and they stand 6.4" and 6" tall. Approximate values vary from $50-$75 each, with the reddish-brown Abyssinian color being the most valuable.

Pasha the baby elephant was produced in the 50s, 60s, and 80s. It stands 3.5" tall and has an approximate value of $40-50.

Rajah the elephant with rider Mahout aboard stands 9.5" tall and was produced in the 50s and 60s. Note the incredible detail in the skin wrinkles on Rajah. Mahout the rider was designed by Nell Bortells. The approximate value of this piece is $160-175, and Rajah alone has an approximate value of $100-120.

Bison has no other name on the Designers' Workshop sales lists. He stands 5.75" tall and was made throughout the 60s, 70s, and early 80s. His brown color and shading varied, as did the color of his mane. His approximate value is $150-175, except for the rare white version that is known to exist.

Geronimo the Brahma bull measures 6" tall and was produced in the 50s and 80s. His approximate value is $90-110.

Hereford cutting steer was issued to go with the cowboy and horse. A similar set is now available in the specialty line, in a smaller scale. This steer was produced in the 50s, 60s, and 80s, and it stands 3.5" tall. The approximate value is $50-60.

Candy the lying Hereford calf is part of a three-way set with brother Dandy and father Domino (not shown). Candy measures 2" tall and was produced in the 50s. Her approximate value is $45-55.

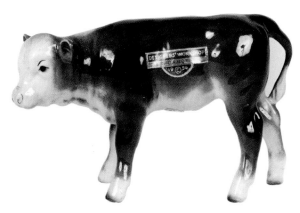

Dandy the standing Hereford calf measures 3" tall. He was produced in the 50s and 60s and has an approximate value of $45-55.

Adelaide the donkey jenny stands 5.25" tall and was made intermittently throughout the 50s, 60s, 70s, and 80s. Her 1" hat was also designed by Maureen Love, and the oldest versions of the hat have flowers on them (as shown). The approximate value for Adelaide alone is $75-100 and for the hat $20-30, with the flowered version being worth more.

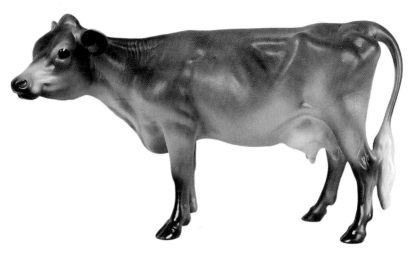

Jersey cow was made in the 80s and stands 5" tall. Her approximate value is $90-100. There is a variation using this mold that has a bonnet and a halo on the cow's head, called Holy Cow, which measures 7" tall and has an approximate value of $120-130.

Harry the donkey foal was made intermittently throughout the 50s, 60s, 70s, and 80s. He stands 3.75" tall and forms a set with Adelaide. His approximate value is $30-40.

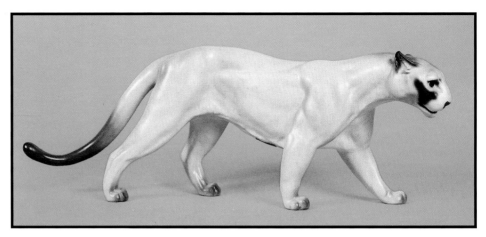

Standing mountain lion was produced in the 50s and 60s with various amounts of shading. This set is relatively light-colored. This lion stands 5.25" tall by 15" long and has an approximate value of $275-300.

Edna the chick is sporting her brother Arthur's name sticker here. Standing 1.8" tall, she was made in the 50s and 60s. Her approximate value is $40-50.

Lying mountain lion is 5" tall by 9" long and was produced in the 50s and 60s. His approximate value is $225-250.

Doe from the early 60s set stands 4.1" tall and has a corresponding buck and fawn (not shown) all in this dark brown color. Her approximate value is $140-150.

This white-tailed doe and fawn were produced in the late 50s. The doe measures 5.5" tall and the fawn is 2.25" tall. There is also a buck with this set (not shown), and they are all considered very rare.

Peggy the walking squirrel measures 4.4" to the top of her out-stretched tail. She was made in brown (shown), gray bisque, and white. Produced in the 60s, her approximate value is $25-30.

Betty the squirrel with acorn was produced in gray bisque (shown), brown, and white. She was made in the 60s and stands 3.25" tall. Her approximate value is $25-30.

Jane is the tallest of the Designers' Workshop squirrels, measuring 5.25". She came in brown (shown) and gray bisque. She was produced throughout the 60s and early 70s and has an approximate value of $60-75.

German Shepherd and Frisbee is a delightful piece that is still in current production. It measures 2.5" tall and has a retail price of $7.

Kudu was in the specialties line for only a short time in the early 90s, perhaps due to breakage. This handsome animal stands 4.25" tall and has an approximate value of $40-45.

This sow was produced in the 80s along with her walking and sitting piglets (not shown). Measuring 3" tall by 7" long, she has an approximate value of $40-45.

The swan was made for a very limited time in the mid-80s. It is 5.75" tall and has an approximate value of $70-75.

Canada goose stands a stately 7.5" tall and was made for only a brief time in the mid-80s. His approximate value is $100-125.

Roadrunner was produced in brown ceramic with wire legs. He stands 4.5" tall and was made during the early 80s. His approximate value is $30-40.

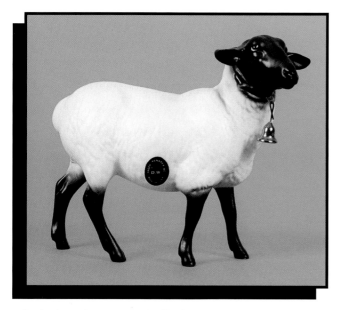

Lady Jane the ewe stands 4" tall and was made in the 50s, 60s, and 80s. The most recent version has a bell attached by a wire (as shown), while the older versions have a bell molded on. Her approximate value is $50-70.

Son John the lamb has been seen with varying amounts of black on the face, from very little (as shown) to a totally black head. He stands 2.75" tall. Produced in the 50s, 60s, and 80s, his approximate value is $35-50.

Nubian doe stands 5" tall and was only produced in the mid-80s. She has two kids that were made at the same time. Her approximate value is $45-50.

Nubian kid walking measures 3" tall. It was produced in the mid-80s with the rest of the family and has an approximate value of $20-25.

Nubian kid standing measures 3" tall. It was produced in the mid-80s and has an approximate value of $20-25.

Koala was produced for less than a year in the mid-80s. He sits 5" tall and has an approximate value of $90-100.

This original sculpture of an Indian and his pony has inspired a production piece that is still currently available on the Hagen-Renaker specialties line. The smaller Indian and pony are 3.8" tall and sell for $20 retail. The wooden base is not original.

This 1974 sculpture is the foal Ibn Nataf, done by Maureen Love during her freelance days when she made things in her own kiln at home. Jim Renaker said that he brought Maureen this clay from Mexico and that she loved to work with it.

The illusive girl and foal statue was to be a part of the A-500 Stoneware series, but never made it into full production. The models for this piece were the daughter of Marlys Klepper, a spray department employee, and a Quarter Horse foal. This Hagen-Renaker model stands 10.8" tall, and the Shirmar version is about an inch taller.

Wonderful examples of Maureen Love's artistic ability are seen on this page from one of her sketchbooks.

This flying pelican demonstrates another area of interest for Maureen Love. Her bird sculptures are just as awesome as her horses. This one measures 10.5" tall and was designed and decorated by her.

One of the first horses produced by Maureen Love is shown here. She designed it, made the mold, produced, fired, and decorated it all at home before she was hired at Hagen-Renaker. When asked what breed this was, Maureen responded that at the time she made it, she was just happy it looked like a horse!

This original sculpture of a Clydesdale stallion was later turned into a production piece in the mid-80s. The factory-produced Clydesdale stands 7.5" tall and has an approximate value of $275-300, but of course this original sculpture is priceless.

Robbie the seated Scottish Terrier puppy measures 2.5" tall and has an approximate value of $40-50.

Mac the adult Scottish Terrier was produced with two puppies in the 50s and 60s. These were some of the few dogs that were not designed by Tom Masterson for the Pedigree Dog line. Mac stands 5.5" tall and has an approximate value of $55-65.

Bonnie the standing Scottish Terrier puppy measures 2.5" tall and has an approximate value of $40-50.

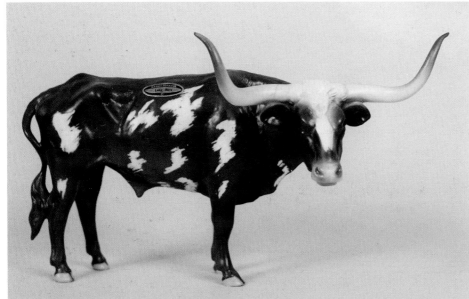

This magnificent longhorn was produced in the early 60s and in the 80s. He was made in this mahogany brown pattern and in light brown. He stands 5.75" tall and has an approximate value of $150-175.

10

Tom Masterson

In an interview conducted in the early 1980's by William Wiemhoff, Tom revealed that he was interested in figures and figurines ever since he was around ten years old, when he first used modeling clay given to him by his mother. He had a year of art training in high school, specializing in working with clay, and also took art classes while in college, as well as a six week art class specializing in clay work at Claremont for his teaching credential in Whittier. The first ceramic he designed was a lettuce leaf salt shaker. He was a business major, and earned his teaching credential in 1948 after graduating from Whittier. According to his wife Bessie P. Masterson, he did not pursue this career because he knew it was just not for him. He loved to work with his hands.

Tom wanted to get into his own pottery work, and he worked for a time in the San Francisco Bay area. Soon after that he was employed by Hagen-Renaker as a designer. According to Jim Renaker, his dad had heard via word of mouth that Tom was a talented carver, so in 1950, John and Jim visited Tom at his home in Duarte to see his work. There they saw soap carvings of sports cars that showed enough talent that they hired him. John Renaker recalls that everybody liked him, but "I was a bit worried, thinking that since he rode an ugly looking motorcycle he might have some psychological problem such as a death wish." Jim recounts that later Tom took a nasty spill on a motorcycle, and that converted him to sports cars.

A few days after John had hired Tom Masterson, Maynard Anthony Freeman applied for a job as a designer. Since Hagen-Renaker couldn't afford to hire two designers, John suggested that he see Jerry McFarlin, which he did, and went on to become very successful as the top designer and partner for Freeman-McFarlin Pottery.

Bill Nicely recalls Tom as a very tall, thin, and dapper fellow. He drove Italian sports cars, after moving up from MG's. He was a very nice guy, but very serious. Maureen Love remembers him as being a very easy-going person that had similar interests to hers.

Almost the entire Pedigree Line of dogs that Hagen-Renaker produced was designed by Tom Masterson. Those dogs are so realistic that they look as if they could jump off the shelf and bark. How then does one account for the "Masterson horses?" Jim Renaker explains that Tom would have done something like that as a cartoon, because he certainly wouldn't have tried to compete with Maureen. So if he were to attempt something like that at all, it would be something kind of different or off the wall. Jim remembers Tom as quite serious and sober. "I don't think he took himself all that serious, but he wasn't really that much of an outgoing person. He was serious in all of his endeavors."

Helen Perrin Farnlund remembers it a little differently. She said that Tom was hired and started designing when the company had grown so big that she couldn't keep up with the demand for new items. Tom was the second designer hired by Hagen-Renaker. At the time that Tom created his horses, Maureen was a decorator. Helen thinks that "the reason Maureen started doing horses was because she saw Tom's horses and she thought they weren't good enough, so she did some. And that was the beginning of her designing." Helen also recalls fondly that the designers "were there together at the pottery, and we were good friends."

Bill contrasts Tom's style of sculpting with Maureen's. Bill explains that there are two different styles of sculpture there. Maureen starts with an armature and builds up. Tom would start with a lump and whittle away. He doesn't recall ever seeing Tom make an armature. He also says that Tom didn't do much in the way of sketching, whereas Maureen sketches a lot. Bill also recalls that Tom's approach to art was that it was just something that he liked to do.

Tom Masterson sculpting a quail in late 1959.

In 1961 Tom, and some of the other designers, were let go. In a letter of recommendation written by John Renaker on February 15, 1961, it was stated "He has proved himself very gifted at this type of work over the years and has to his credit many commercially successful models and lines. We would, if we could, keep him working for us. His leaving will hurt us in our future development of new products, and we would not lose his help if we could afford to do otherwise."

Prior to working for Hagen-Renaker, Tom served in the Navy during World War II, stationed in Willow Grove, Pennsylvania. His title was Specialist and he worked on the fuel systems of C-47 and A-26 aircraft and had to plan repair manuals for engine systems. He then went to work for Douglas Aircraft in Long Beach, California, as a Technical Illustrator, working with blueprints, and transferring information into perspective and isometric illustrations for field maintenance personnel to use.

After leaving Hagen-Renaker, Tom went to work for Scott Aviation, formerly known as Sierra Engineering. Tom's first project at that company in 1962 was development of a heart valve under a Hartford Grant. He was manager of the pattern and design shop. In that capacity, Tom and his crew developed the anatomy dummies, Sim 1, 2, and 3. These figures were used at USC for medical seminary, because they were so life-like with throat and tongue very real to the touch. He also helped create realistic crash dummies with bones that broke and skin that suffered lacerations so that after the crash the dummy could be put on a table for an "autopsy."

This dummy was known to the auto industry as "Sophisticated Sam." In addition, Tom lent his expertise to the development of medical and military oxygen systems as well as numerous helmets, and a glue used for quick stitches. This information comes from the Scott Aviation newsletter that announced his retirement in its June/July 1986 issue.

His wife Bessie also mentioned that he worked on molds for the Hot Wheels™ automobiles, trucks, and other vehicles for Mattel. She and Tom were married in August, 1955. She describes him as a person who enjoyed experimenting with all kinds of materials, including wood, bisque, porcelain, and metal. He had built his own little house where he spent many hours working on models and finishing them in his own ovens. She said that they still refer to the house as "Uncle Tom's house."

Tom also loved music and as a result accumulated quite a library of classical, jazz, and instrumental music. He favored Benny Goodman and all the melodies of the 20s and 30s. He also enjoyed reading, and had a library of books on ceramics, history, art, animals, automobiles and other topics. His mind and interests in everything never stopped. He was a warm, compassionate, and religious man. Bessie also mentioned how much he respected the talents of Maureen, Helen, and Nell, and how grateful he was for his association with the Renaker family. He appreciated the opportunity to work with such outstanding, talented individuals during that period of his life. Tom passed away August 17, 1986.

A silver sculpture that Tom did for his wife Bessie Masterson.

Rearing horse was produced in the early 50s in palomino and bay. It stands 5.5" tall and has an approximate value of $75-80.

Head down foal stands 2" tall and was made in bay (shown) and palomino. It was made in the early 50s and has an approximate value of $50-60.

Half-rearing horse was produced in the early 50s in palomino and bay (shown). It stands 5" tall and has an approximate value of $80-100.

These are examples of some of the Masterson miniature horses. They also came in prancing poses and a reclining pose. The adult on the left is the feet together saddle horse which came in palomino and bay and stands 2.4" tall. The colt on the right also came in bay and palomino and is 1.75" tall. They were made in the early 50s and their approximate values are $40-45 for the saddle horse and $20-25 for the colt.

Head up foal was produced in bay and palomino (shown). It was produced in the early 50s and has an approximate value of $50-60.

Von the German Shepherd was made in the 50s and early 60s. He stands 6" tall and has an approximate value of $60-75.

Mitzi the German Shepherd puppy has a sibling named Fritzi, who is in a begging pose. Mitzi is 3" tall and was made in the 50s and early 60s. Her approximate value is $55-60.

Gypsy the Airdale was produced in the late 50s, then intermittently in the 60s and 70s. It stands 3" tall and has an approximate value of $45-55.

Baron the German Shepherd stands 3.25" tall and was made in the 50s, 60s and 80s. His approximate value is $25-45, with the older pieces being the most valuable.

Hamlet the incredible Great Dane looks great in either his fawn color or this harlequin pattern. He is 4.5" tall, and was produced in the 50s and 60s. This particular model is one of the older ones, as he does not have an incised spot pattern. The fawn colored dog has an approximate value of $80-100 and the harlequin is worth approximately $200-250.

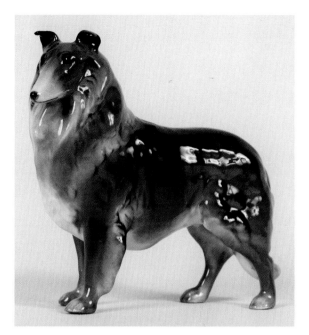

Laddie the Collie puppy is 2.5" tall. He came in brown and white or brown, black and white, and was made in the mid-50s. His approximate value is $40-45.

Golden Lady the Collie was only produced in the mid-50s. She stands 6" tall and 8" long, and has an approximate value of $80-90.

Gaylord the small style standing Collie came with a mate Bonnie. Made in the 50s, 60s, and 70s, Gaylord stands 3.4" tall and has an approximate value of $50-70.

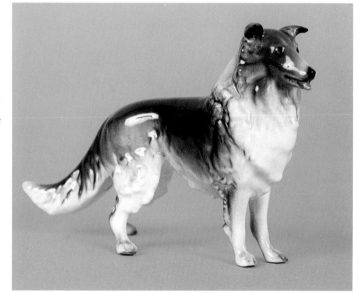

Bonnie the small style lying Collie was produced in the 50s, 60s, and 70s. She is 2" tall and has an approximate value of $40-45.

Fifi the poodle was made in gray and white (shown). She stands 5" tall and was produced in the late 50s and early 60s. Her approximate value is $65-75.

Ralph the Poodle puppy is Fifi's puppy. He stands 2" tall and was only produced in the early 60s, in white. He has an approximate value of $40-45.

Yvonne the Poodle stands 3" tall and was produced in white (shown) and gray. She was made in the 50s and 60s and has an approximate value of $60-70.

Cecil the Poodle was made intermittently in the 60s. He stands 4" tall and was produced in white and gray. His approximate value is $60-70.

Patsy the Cocker Spaniel puppy normally is found in the tan color on the left. However, the white puppy with red-brown freckles is a rare variation. Patsy stands 2.75" tall and was produced in the 50s and 60s. The approximate value on the tan version is $25-35.

Honey Girl the Cocker Spaniel is Patsy's mom. Produced in the 50s and 60s, Honey Girl stands 5.5" tall and has an approximate value of $35-45.

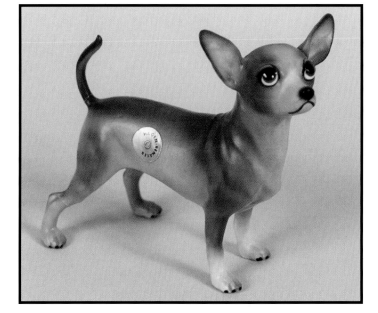

Carmencita the Chihuahua was made in the 50s and 60s. She stands 4.25" tall and has an approximate value of $40-50.

Pancho Villa is the puppy of Carmecita, and the stickers for these two were frequently switched (shown here). The puppy is 2" tall and was produced in the 50s and 60s. He has an approximate value of $20-25.

Spooky the seated Dalmatian measures 5.5" and was made during the 50s and 60s. His approximate value is $55-70.

Spooky the lying Dalmatian shares the same name with his seated companion. The lying Spooky measures 2.5" tall and was produced in the late 50s and early 60s. The approximate value is $50-60.

Choo Choo the Pekinese puppy was produced in the late 50s and early 60s. It stands 2" tall and has an approximate value of $30-35.

Vicki the smooth-haired Fox Terrier came in two versions, white-faced (shown) or with a black face. She was made in the late 50s and briefly in the 60s and stands 4.5" tall. Her approximate value is $90-100.

Ming Toy is the adult Pekinese that goes with Choo Choo, and was made intermittently during the 50s and 60s. It stands 3" tall and has an approximate value of $40-50.

Mickey the Pomeranian was made intermittently throughout the 50s and 60s. He stands 3.5" tall and has an approximate value of $40-50.

Pip Emma the Cocker Spaniel was only made in the mid-50s. She is 2.5" tall and has an approximate value of $35-40.

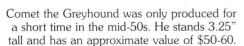

His Nibs the Cocker Spaniel came in both tan and black and white (both versions shown). He stands 2.5" tall and was produced intermittently throughout the 50s, 60s, 70s, and 80s. His approximate value is $25-30.

Mops the Old English Sheepdog came with varying amounts of gray shading from very little (as shown) to much more than this. The black and white version of this mold was used as Disney's Shaggy Dog in the late 50s. Mops was produced in the 50s, 60s, and 70s and sits 3.5" tall. The approximate value is $35-55, with the black and white version being the most valuable.

Comet the Greyhound was only produced for a short time in the mid-50s. He stands 3.25" tall and has an approximate value of $50-60.

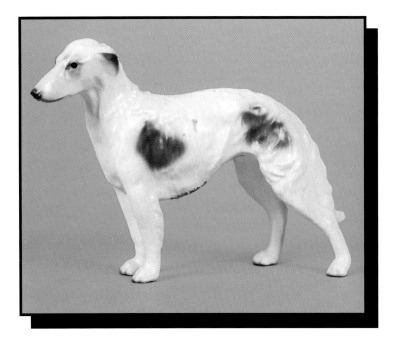

Russian Wolfhound has no name, which is unusual for the Pedigree Dog line. He stands 3.6" tall and was only briefly produced in the 50s and 60s. His approximate value is $50-60.

Helga the standing Doberman Pinscher was produced in the 50s and 60s and stands 5.8" tall. She has an approximate value of $90-95.

Friar the Saint Bernard came in a variety of shades of brown, from tan to this very dark brown on white. He was made intermittently throughout the 50s, 60s, and 70s and measures 2.5" tall. His approximate value is $45-50.

Diana the sitting Doberman Pinscher is Helga's companion and measures 5.75" tall. She was produced in the 50s and 60s and has an approximate value of $90-95.

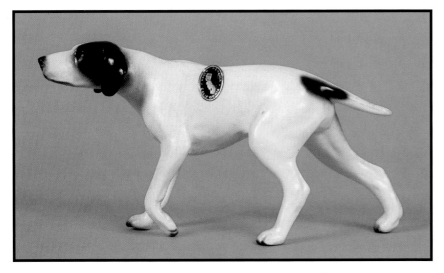

This Pointer mold was used for other breeds as well. In this brown spotted version it was the Pointer, in solid brown it was the German Pointer, and in tan is was the Vizsla. This dog was made in the late 60s, and stands 3" tall. The approximate value is $50-55.

Manchester Terrier was produced in black and tan (shown) and in a reddish color. He stands 3" tall and was made intermittently in the 50s, 60s, and 70s. He has an approximate value of $55-65.

Blue Boy the Weimaraner was produced in the late 50s and 60s. He stands 5" tall and has an approximate value of $70-75.

Monicle the Afghan Hound stands 4" tall and sports a breed sticker. He was made in the 50s and 70s and has an approximate value of $45-55.

Squire the English Setter has a name and date sticker. This mold was also produced in a reddish brown and called an Irish Setter. Squire stands 5.25" tall and was made in the mid-50s. His approximate value is $65-75.

Bernie the Dachshund measures 6.5" tall and 14" long. He was produced in the 50s and 60s and has an approximate value of $150-175.

This next group of dogs exemplifies some of the most awesome work created by Hagen-Renaker. Leading off this group of large-scale dogs is Lady the Dalmatian, who measures 10" and has incredible detail. She was made in the 50s and 60s and has an approximate value of $175-200.

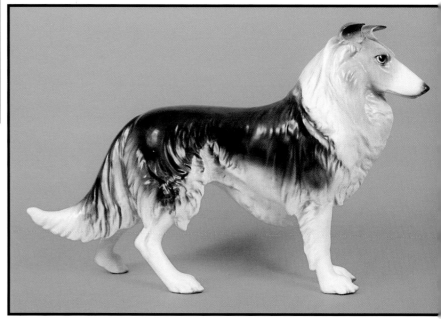

Gaylord the large Collie came in varying shades of brown and white. He stands 10" tall and was produced in the 50s and 60s. He has an approximate value of $150-175.

Maggie the Boxer is the tallest dog at a height of 11.5". She is the only large dog who has a puppy, Champ. Maggie was produced in the 50s and 60s and has an approximate value of $150-175.

Champ the Boxer puppy is 5.25" tall. He was produced in the 50s and 60s and has an approximate value of $45-50.

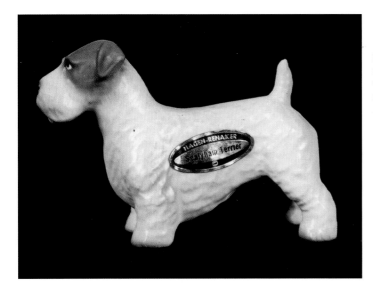

Sealyham Terrier had no other name on the order forms. He stands 2" tall, was briefly produced in the 50s and 60s, and has an approximate value of $40-50.

Nobby the English Bulldog puppy forms a set with sibling Bobby and daddy Winston. Nobby is 1.75" tall and was produced in the 50s and 60s. He has an approximate value of $35-40.

Chester the Boston Terrier puppy (left) was only produced briefly in the mid-50s. In the 60s the mold was reused to produce this Boxer puppy (right). Sitting 2.25" tall, their approximate values are $70-75 for the black and white puppy and $40-45 for the fawn-colored one.

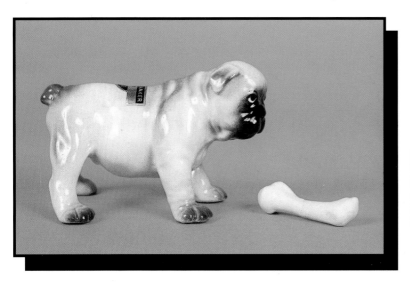

Bobby stands 2" tall and is posed here with a bone that actually forms a set with one of the Boxers, Princess. Bobby was produced in the mid-50s only and has an approximate value of $40-50. The bone is 1.5" long, was also made in the mid-50s, and is considered rare.

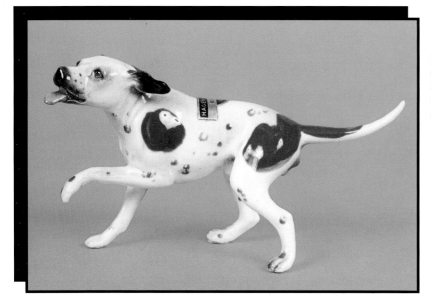

Ranger the running Pointer came in solid black with tan, and in this white with red or black spots. Standing 2.5" tall, he was made in the 50s and 60s. His approximate value is $55-70, with the solid black version being worth more.

Sam the crouching Beagle puppy was also issued for a short time as a Dalmatian named Flint. Sam measures 2.25" tall at tail tip and was produced in the 50s and 60s. His approximate value is $35-40, and as a Dalmatian is $45-50.

Sally the Beagle stands 5" tall. She was made in the 50s and 60s and has an approximate value of $50-60.

Belle the Beagle and her puppy Beau were produced for a very limited time in the late 50s and are considered rare. Hagen-Renaker released other Beagles in the Pedigree Dogs line with these same names. Belle measures 3.75" tall and Beau is 1.6" tall.

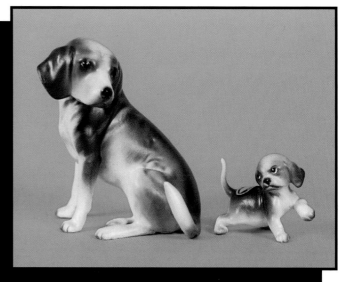

Dutchess the Boxer was only made in the late 50s. She measures 3.25" tall and has an approximate value of $45-55.

King the Boxer puppy sits 1.5" tall and was produced in the late 50s and early 60s. His approximate value is $30-35.

Benny the Basset Hound came in varying patterns of black, brown, and white. He is 4.5" tall at the tail tip by 6.25" long, and was produced in the 50s and 60s. He has an approximate value of $55-65.

Bloodhound was produced in two different colors. The reddish-brown version (shown) is the older one, and he also came in light brown with a dark brown pattern. He is 2.6" tall and was produced briefly in the 50s, 60s, and 70s. His approximate value is $40-55, with the reddish-brown ones being more valuable.

Miniature standing Collie was produced with a varying amount of black shading. Measuring 1.5" tall, this Collie was made from the 50s through the 90s. His approximate value is $4-12.

This duo of circus dogs were part of the circus set. Both are 2" tall, were produced in the mid-50s, and have an approximate value of $20-25. The pedestals they are standing on have an approximate value of $12-15.

Pom Pom the walking kitten is usually found in Siamese or tabby coloring. This calico kitten is a very rare color variation. Pom Pom is 3" tall and was made in the late 50s and 60s. Its approximate value is $40-50 for the usual colors.

This charming miniature donkey family was produced from the 50s until the 70s. They were available in both gray and tan, and some of the older pieces have holes in their mouths for flowers (flowers shown are not original). Baby stands 1.6" tall, and the adults are 2.25" tall. Baby has an approximate value of $7-10, and Mama (seated) and Papa (standing) have an approximate value of $10-15.

Choo San the Siamese cat sits a towering 10.75" tall. He has a similar looking companion Ching Li which measures 7" tall. Choo San was produced intermittently in the 50s, 60s, and 70s and has an approximate value of $35-45.

This lying Persian cat was only made for a brief time in the mid-50s. It measures 5" tall by 9.75" long and has an approximate value of $90-100.

Fuzzy the begging cat came in two colors, the Siamese (shown) and in a striped tabby color. He stands 4.75" tall and was made in the late 50s. His approximate value is $45-50.

The Siamese tail-watching cat is 3" tall and was produced in the early 50s. It has an approximate value of $45-55.

Moonbeam the crouched Persian kitten was made throughout the 50s and 60s. She is 3.8" tall at tail tip and has an approximate value of $25-30.

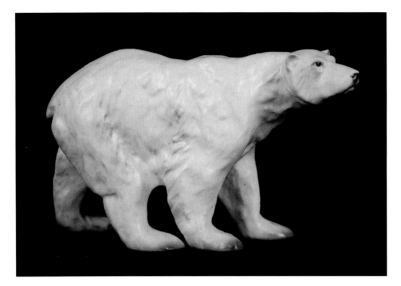

Polar Bear has no name, which is unusual for Designers' Workshop animals. He stands 3.75" tall and was produced in the 60s. He has an approximate value of $150-175.

Cartoony elephant mama was produced in the early 50s with two baby elephants that closely resemble her in color and detail. She measures 5" tall and has an approximate value of $50-60.

Timothy the mouse was produced in brown, gray, and white. The hat that was designed for Adelaide the donkey fits him perfectly. He stands 2.5" tall (without hat) and was produced in the 50s, 60s, 70s, and 80s. His approximate value is $20-30.

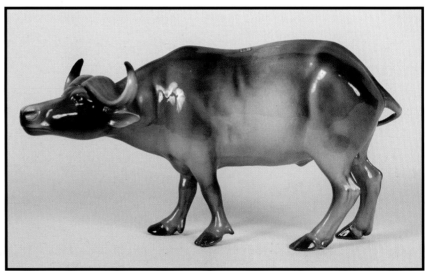

Cape Buffalo was made for a very brief time in the mid-50s. He stands 4.75" tall and 9" long. He has an approximate value of $275-300.

Quail, standing, measures 5" tall to the top of his feather. This represents the more common color for this bird, but he has also been found in gray. He was produced intermittently in the 50s, 60s, and 70s, and has an approximate value of $40-50.

This pheasant is the short-legged version made by Hagen-Renaker. A similar bird with longer legs in a walking pose was designed by Maureen Love. This pheasant measures 5.25" tall and was produced in the early 50s. He has an approximate value of $70-75.

Bighorn sheep on a rock slab base was produced in white (shown) and tan. It was made intermittently throughout the 60s, 70s, and 80s. It stands 7.25" tall and has an approximate value of $150-175.

This impish baby raccoon has a hole in his hand to hold flowers. He stands 1.5" tall and was made in this color during the early 50s. He has an approximate value of $6-8.

"You know, you have to be pretty spunky to be an artist and try to make a living these days. It's not an easy way to go." These words were spoken by Nell to describe Martha Armstrong Hand, but they could just as well be used to describe her. Always an artist, no matter what she was involved in, and with a slightly "warped" (her word) sense of humor as she enjoyed the world and people around her.

Nell explains,

At the time that I graduated from high school, which is in 1944, there were three art schools in Los Angeles. One was Art Center, another was the Otis Art Institute, and there was Chouinard Art Institute. I met Mrs. Chouinard when she had come to our high school to speak to our art club, and she had seen some of my work. All I ever wanted to do was be an artist. I won a full scholarship, so that's where I went to school.

I didn't have any training as far as ceramics is concerned. But after I left Chouinard, I was painting. I got a job in Yosemite, and got to thinking about things. Then when I got home, I painted. My mother and aunt had known John Renaker when he was a little boy. In fact, my mother taught him how to swim and he never forgot that. They heard that John and Maxine had this new business going, and they said to me 'Why don't you go down and apply for a job? They need somebody, because one of the decorators is sick, and you can earn some Christmas money.' I thought OK, I'll just go down and do that, but I was there for over eleven years!

I started out as a decorator. In fact, it was while I was doing decorating, and during a coffee break, I had a piece of wet clay, and I made a mouse about the same size as your fingernail, and the tail was sticking out. John walked by and saw it, and he said 'Where did that come from?' I said I just made it, and he said can I have it? I said sure. And he came back with a check for $25! Then he had a mold made of the little mouse. I thought gee, that was easy! So I quickly made a teeny little piece of cheese and he came back with a check for $10 for me. So every once in a while I would do some things. I also got involved in setting up decorating for all the critters after a while. The pottery just grew. When I started working there it was really kind of the beginning, around 1948.

This tiny mouse was the beginning of design work for Nell Bortells at Hagen-Renaker. Measuring .6" tall, this little critter was in production from the early 50s through the 70s and has an approximate value of $5-10. His companion piece of cheese has an approximate value of $5-8.

I would do the samples for the shows. It was always hurry up, hurry up, sometimes I was firing in little test kilns all night to get samples for the shows. These samples were often finished up in just the last few days before the big shows, which were important in those days for our first big orders, and they would help to kick start the salesmen.

John Renaker has commented that the reason Hagen-Renaker kept producing this large cat by Don Winton for so long was because of the beautiful job Nell did decorating the face.

Nell Bortells at a 50s Christmas party in the Hagen-Renaker factory.

Eventually they put me in charge of the decorating department. Helen was doing designs at that time. Maxine of course did their initial designs. And John's mother, Moss Renaker. When John wanted to start Designers' Workshop, he wanted me to start it. He said that I could take a certain number of people up there, a couple of decorators, a couple of mold people, and so forth. So I chose key people that I thought would be good for it, and we started Designers' Workshop. Helen did a few of our things for Designers' Workshop, but mostly it was Maureen and Tom.

I had a chance to possibly go to Europe, and as an artist that appealed to me. So I told John I thought I wanted to go overseas, and be an artist, I guess. The next morning he called and invited me to go out for breakfast, and he said he had just gotten the Disney contract. He wondered if I would be interested in just doing designing. So as a group he took us over to the Disney Studios, and there I met Walt Disney himself. He took us through the studio. It was quite a wonderful experience. I did the original Seven Dwarves, the large ones, for Designers' Workshop. I went across the street to Moss Renaker's place, as I had a room there and felt very comfortable, and I just designed away. They sent home a film with me so I could keep referring to it, and I turned out the Seven Dwarves.

The dwarf Dopey stands 3.1" tall and was produced in the late 50s. His approximate value is $175-200. Snow White was designed by Don Winton, stands 5.75" tall, and has an approximate value of $275-300

Left to right are the dwarfs Grumpy, Sneezy, and Happy. They are 3.25" tall, were produced in the late 50s, and have approximate values of $175-200 each.

Left to right are the dwarfs Bashful, Sleepy, and Doc. The first two stand 3.4" tall and Doc is 3.6" tall. Produced in the late 50s, they have an approximate value of $175-200 each.

Special sticker used for the Hagen-Renaker ceramics that were Walt Disney productions.

Soon, the pottery was having problems, so they closed down the designer thing. A few of us got together and tried to make a go at our own business, McAfee's. Most of the others worked at it at night or on the week ends, but because I wasn't prepared to go back as a decorator, and because they already had someone to take over managing the decorating department, I was put in charge of that company. I think we lasted for about a year. Then I finally had to go get a job, so that's when I left the pottery business.

I went up and down the streets looking for a job, because I had used up every bit of my savings trying to get through the McAfee's thing, to make that pay. And I swore I was never going to depend upon art to make a living. I got a job as a cashier at the telephone company, then I became a customer representative. They trained you to have the answers, so people would call in upset or angry, and you had solutions to their problems so it was very satisfying. I could talk 8 hours a day, which seemed like a good way to go. But all the time I worked, wherever I worked, I always used my art instincts. Like, I ended up doing lots of decorating for the contests and the office. I retired around 1987. My mom had had a stroke, and I was up there about 3 times a day, so I retired and took a pension.

The Little Horribles are definitely my favorite pieces I've made. It started in the late 1950s when John asked me to make a vulture for the miniature line. I made a fat, cute, cheerful little vulture, and John said 'No, a HUNGRY vulture!' I was so dumbfounded, because normally my approach to things is a little more like the hungry vulture, but I tried very hard to make cheerful critters. So then I made a hungry vulture that looked like it was really ready to rip your heart out, and he took it and made a mold of it. His idea was, well, he also had this kind of a sense of humor that this would make a nice gift to send to someone in the hospital. That amused me too; I thought that was funny. Then he wanted some more things in the same style, and that's when the Little Horribles started. I made that little green, hairy man, a cave for him, a little blue kid for a friend, and a little froggy, toady monstery-looking thing for his pet. I think everybody, even ugly

people, deserve to have friends and pets. John's approach to humor was my kind of humor, so they appealed to me. But I did not come up with the name 'Horribles.' He came up with that name, and it really kind of offended me because by that time they were my little friends, my little critters, and I didn't see them as horrible. However it is a good, catchy name. And it was kind of fun to have something that I enjoyed doing and that seemed a little more natural to my whatever kind of humor it is. Warped is a pretty good description of it, I guess."

Little Horribles vultures. The larger one may not be a production piece, but the smaller one is 1.8" tall, was produced in the late 50s, and has an approximate value of $50-60.

The eye spider was specifically designed to fit into the bumps on the cave for display purposes. Eye spider is .8" tall and has an approximate value of $60-65. The cave is 3.25" tall and has an approximate value of $60-65. The little old man stands 2" tall and has an approximate value of $50-55.

Due to the popularity at that time of the Purple People Eater song, Nell was inspired to design her own version of the Purple People Eater. It stands 1.25" tall, was produced in the late 50s, and has an approximate value of $70-75.

Here are three examples of the warped Little Horribles. Tycoon sits 1.8" tall and has an approximate value of $55-60. Footsore and Weary is 1.6" at the highest point and has an approximate value of $50-55. Horse Laugh is 2.5" tall and has an approximate value of $50-55.

A historical note; in 1969, Nell served on the jury that convicted Sirhan Sirhan of the murder of Robert F. Kennedy. Nell still works with Susan Nikas on occasional projects for the miniature and specialty lines. Nell was especially helpful in teaching Susan about techniques that were used with the Little Horribles, such as the special glazes, and the multi-part molds. Nell also enjoys her little Yorkie, "Sophie Tucker, the last of the Red Hot Mamas," a former breeder's dog. She says Sophie "loves to go for rides, so I put a bunch of pillows on the passenger's side so she can look directly out the window. She looks like Cleopatra going down the Nile on her barge." Quite the spunky duo driving the streets of Monrovia!

Tommy the Tortoise and Harry the Hare are from the famous fable. Tommy and Harry both measure 1.5" tall, were produced in the mid-50s, and have an approximate value of $150-175 each.

Albert the curbstone setter (left) was produced in the early 60s. This mold was later used in the 80s to produce a dog simply known as Mutt (right). Measuring 2.75" tall, Albert has an approximate value of $35-45 and Mutt has an approximate value of $20-25.

These miniature puppies were only known as lying puppy and seated puppy. The lying one is .5" tall and the seated one is 1.25" tall. They were produced for a short time in the mid-50s, and their approximate value is $15-18 each.

Caterpillar Ma and Pa were produced from the 50s until the 80s. Pa sometimes had a pipe in his mouth, and Ma's bonnet color varied, with blue being the most common. Ma measures 1" tall and Pa is 1.25" tall. Their approximate value is $5-10 each.

Mr Froggie is .6" tall and was produced from the 80s until the present. His current retail price is $3.

Dancing frogs have been in the specialty line since the early 90s. They are 3.5" tall and sell for a retail price of $16.

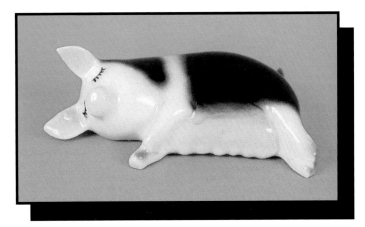

Pig mama nursing has been in the miniature line since the early 80s. She has a family of piglets and a papa pig that go with her. She is 1" tall and has a current retail price of $4.50.

Examples of dogs from the Curbstone Setter series that were designed and decorated by Nell Bortells.

The Mad Hatter from Alice in Wonderland, as designed and decorated by Nell Bortells.

12

Martha Armstrong Hand

Martha certainly wins the prize for the most variety in her life. She has lived in Europe, faced the struggles of being a Jewish person in Germany during World War II, and fled successfully to the United States to make a life for herself and her family. At age 79 she continues to live an active and stimulating life, filled with art and joy.

In her own words,

I was born in Berlin, Germany. My first figures I made at age twelve were story telling devices. I loved all crafts; paper folding, macramé, and later book binding and lettering. At age 17 I became an apprentice to a wood carver at the Academy of Arts in Berlin, and I adored Romanic and early Gothic carving. I had always been fond of animal sculpture. I took a class with a zoo professor and spent a whole summer drawing oxen and donkeys at the Berlin Zoo! At the Academy of Arts in Berlin I was an eager student. As an apprentice, I was allowed to take night classes. I took everything I could lay my hands on: figure drawing, pose drawing, anatomy (both animal and human). As a student I took advantage of all the crafts offered: ceramic, bookbinding, porcelain painting, and more.

When I was thrown out of the Academy of Arts in Berlin because of my Jewish ancestry I managed to have a short apprenticeship in a graphic arts studio. There I discovered my love and gift for lettering and I spent a year there, lettering like a monk (tuning out the war and nightly bomb attacks). The end of the war was spent as a map drawing apprentice.

After a flight from the Nazis and finally the Russian Army, I was able to use my various skills living on a farm in northern Germany. The wood carving was used making dolls, puppets and some decorative furniture carving as an exchange for food and useful furniture. The lettering also came in handy for a job doing sign writing for the British Army of occupation. While doing that I met a bombardier, Sam, who later became my husband. After the war, we married and finally immigrated to the United States. This was in 1949.

Arts were put on hold as I held various positions, from ranch hand, chicken rancher, decoration chairman for a local organization, craft teacher at several schools, and finally a turn of events that became a unique moment in my life. During a summer camp, I was introduced to the father of a new student, who was impressed with my puppets and said 'I need someone to sew for me, I am making puppets for View Master.™' Oh, this was the magic word. I had View Master slides in my house and the children and I were fond of them. Here was a man who offered me a job...sewing?!! I really had not sewn since high school and then we did a pillowcase which took me the full semester. But the wheels turned in my head, I saw myself making puppets for View Master! So of course I said yes. I got a contract and the story he was working on turned out to be *2000 Leagues Under the Sea*. Somehow I pulled it off, don't ask me how.

I no longer worked for the school, as by now the school required credentials from every teacher. I rented a booth in an arts and crafts market thinking of creating puppets for sale. I was so taken by my environment that I did more watching than working. In the meantime the scenic artist from View Master came for a visit with the news that I was invited to try out as a sculptor for *The Ten Commandments*. When that project was canceled I took a job lettering at a greeting card company. This was a hard test, as speed was expected from everybody. But happily View Master came through for me with first *Rudolph the Red Nose Reindeer Shines Again*, and later *Bambi*.

Martha busily working on a scene from *Bambi* at View Master.

The figures must have been successful, as a license supervisor of Disney saw them and recommended me to the ceramic company of Hagen-Renaker. Mr. Renaker offered me a job and an agreement was reached in which I could work at home and bring my designs to Monrovia once a week. I was paid a salary. This was a great step as I now could afford to buy a car!

I started work for Renaker in 1957. It was a good business, but as a result of being copied in the Orient it almost went out of business. Mr. Renaker experimented with licensing Disney and larger figures like a cat and kittens, a chipmunk with babies, four South Sea Gods, and even a young lady (teenager). I learned mold making at Renakers. We always had to do the first mold so we wouldn't make such a complicated piece that needed endless molds. What a sensible idea! Can you imagine. For a designer to go through the process of mold making, to understand it. We did not make the final mold, though; they had a special mold shop.

Sleeping Beauty set designed by Martha Armstrong in the late 50s. The items in this incredible set include, from left, King Stefan, Queen, King Hubert, Flora, Fauna, Merryweather, Samson the horse, Prince Phillip, Sleeping Beauty, red Cardinal, Bluebird, Maleficent, Rabbit, Squirrel, and Owl. The people range from 2" to 2.8" tall and are worth approximately $175-200 each. Maleficent is the exception at an approximate value of $700-750. The birds are .5" tall and the other animals are 1-2" tall, with a value of approximately $40-50. The exception is Samson the horse who stands 2.75" tall and has an approximate value of $700-750.

This set of Snow White and the Seven Dwarfs is referred to as the smaller one, since it is a smaller scale than the set designed by Nell Bortells. This set was produced in the late 50s and features (from left) Sneezy, Bashful, Doc, Sleepy, Snow White, Dopey, Grumpy, and Happy. Snow White stands 2.25" tall and the dwarfs are 1.1" to 1.4" tall except for Sleepy who is .4" tall. The approximate value for the dwarfs is $50-60 each, and for Snow White $110-115.

The four South Sea Gods were never mass produced by Hagen-Renaker, perhaps because their style was so different from the other items being produced.

This teenage girl was made for consideration, but was never mass produced by Hagen-Renaker. She measures 7" tall.

I was laid off in 1959 due to the effect of the Oriental competition. The experimentation with the animals (bear and ape) were done later, about 1960, when I was free lancing. The bear and the ape were a new treat. I spent two days in the San Diego Zoo simply observing these creatures and then went home to model roughly in clay, then in wax. I remember spending a whole night building up the wax of the bear thinking about the essentials of nature. It was a very special experience!

I was in love with all of the animals. I wouldn't have gone into great anatomical detail of the bear or the ape, but would come out with something very simplified that would capture the spirit and the motion of it. For the set of three large cats, I went to a cattery, where they keep the cats when someone is on vacation and drew there for a whole day or more. I never did anything unless I studied it.

Since that time, I've done more with View Master (*Bugs Bunny*, *Woody Woodpecker*, and *The Night Before Christmas* among others),

worked as a costume sewer for the Bob Baker Marionette Theater, worked for a baker making sugar decorations for cakes, and then worked for 20 years with Mattel, as a doll maker and sculptor. Now I make dolls on my own that are known for their realism. In order to develop the joints that my dolls now have, I had to be completely in charge as designer, engineer and crafter.

The coast is five minutes from my house down the hill. I saw Cambria with a friend (about 20 years ago now) and within 6 weeks I moved—but—I had a contract with Mattel...Two months later this gentleman (20 years older than I) walks into my rented studio and introduces himself as David Hand, Director of *Snow White* and *Bambi*, and wants to work with me for *Sesame Street*. Well, it turned out I am not a puppeteer (as he thought) 'just' a sculptor of puppets...so—we got married instead. I had dreamt of an 8 cornered house with a loft in the middle. Instead David had this little cabin with 7' ceilings (he was 6'2"). We had to build on to find room for *my* things.

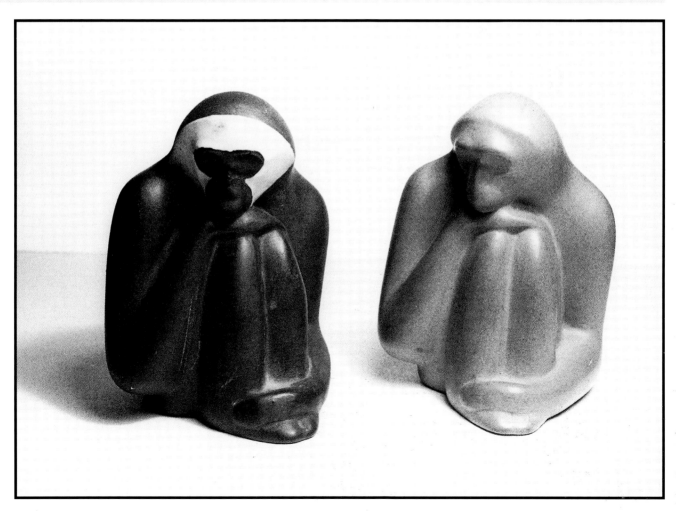

This ape and the corresponding bear were made in the same abstract style. The ape measures 3.3" tall, and was never mass-produced by Hagen-Renaker.

Martha's zest for life is evident, whether speaking with her or enjoying her artwork. She continues to make dolls and conduct master doll-making classes. Although her tenure at Hagen-Renaker was only for a few years, she remembers that period fondly. Martha comments, "The Renakers are very special people and have a very warm spot in my memory."

This papa fluffy cat or Persian was made in two styles. The one as shown with the tail wrapped around the body was produced in the 60s, and with the tail extended out from the body in the late 50s. It was also made seated on a ceramic pillow. The cat is 1.75" tall and the approximate value is $15-25, with the older version and the version seated on the pillow being the most valuable.

The snowy owl mama and baby were produced from the late 50s through the early 70s. The mama is 1.4" tall and the baby is .75" tall. Their approximate values are $7-10 for the mama and $4-6 for the baby.

Both this Poodle adult and puppy were produced in gray (shown), white, and for a brief time in the mid-60s in pink. They were made from the late 50s through the late 70s, and their approximate values are $10-12 for the adult and $8-10 for the puppy, with the pink one being the most valuable.

Squirrel mama with paw up was produced in gray and varying shades of brown. She was made intermittently during the 50s, 60s, 70s, and 80s, and stands 1.5" tall. Her approximate value is $8-10.

Cottontail mama has been produced in varying shades of brown, pale yellow, and white, from the late 50s through the late 80s. The facial detail and toenails on this one identifies it as one of the earliest ones. She stands 1.5" tall and has an approximate value of $6-15.

Starlite the sitting Persian cat and her kittens were designed by Martha after she spent some time at a cattery (where cats were boarded) studying the feline residents. Starlite is 6.5" tall, was produced in the 50s, 60s, and 70s, and has an approximate value of $35-45.

Glitter the sitting Persian kitten came in marmalade orange or white (shown). She is in a set with her playmate Sparkle, and they can be posed batting at each other. Glitter is 3.25" tall, was produced in the 50s, 70s, and 80s, and has an approximate value of $25-30.

Sparkle the lying Persian kitten was produced in white or marmalade orange (both colors shown), and measures 2.25" high. She was produced in the 50s, 70s, and 80s, and has an approximate value of $25-30.

This duo is titled "Motherhood Now and Then, 1884," and was produced by Martha in 1984. This is an example of the porcelain dolls that she still creates.

13

Pat O'Brien Kristof

A name unfamiliar to collectors, but a significant person in the company's development, Pat O'Brien Kristof worked in the early 50s as a decorator, and later as the head of the decorating department for the Designers' Workshop.

As Pat explains,

My first exposure to the pottery business was in 1945 when my Girl Scout troop took a tour through the Walker Pottery. John Renaker was with our troop when we were escorted through. I found out later from Nell that he was actually out there training to be a potter, and that his mother was working there. I fell in love with pottery and all the processes it went through.

Later, I answered an ad in the paper that said that the pottery was looking for decorators. I didn't have any formal training in art before going to work for Hagen-Renaker. I always got A's in art all through grade school and high school, but Maxine did not know this. She actually asked me to write my full name out. And that's how she judged, I guess, how someone was artistic, with their signature. This was her way of separating the ones that scribbled and ones that didn't.

I was hired February 22, 1949, as a decorator. Designers' Workshop started the latter part of 1950 or January 1951. Nell and I were decorators, and she chose me to go with her to start up the Designers' Workshop decorating department. Nell designed all the time that I worked as her assistant. She just decided to finally make me department head when she went into designing full time. We worked together, but mostly they worked back and forth between the spraying department and the designers to accomplish the look that they wanted. I was Nell's assistant for two years before being given the title, but I was doing the actual job of supervisor the whole time, so the job didn't change really when Nell left.

Patsy O'Brien, now Kristof, sitting on the brick wall in front of Designers' Workshop in 1953.

I helped the girls out, unkinked any problems, and I also trained the new ones. If they were having trouble with their paint, if when they were painting an animal, sometimes if you put it on too heavy then it would flake up and off. They'd have to deal with that. Sometimes the little paint pots would dry up and they didn't realize it, and you'd have to stir it deep, so you would have to help them. This was for newer people. And the right brush to use for the right item. We did a lot with sizes of brushes, from 00 to 6. I actually just sat with a new decorator and painted one of the easier animals. Then gradually brought in harder to paint animals, and some of them just started out well and moved right along. Others didn't, but they could produce a lot, their quotas. There were three ways to go...out the door, meet the production quota, or there were the ones that were super good that they used in the shows. I could probably tell you, all of my animals were taken to shows. I'll do a little bragging there.

This miniature mama cow was one of the first pieces Pat decorated. It was designed by Helen Perrin Farnlund. The cow measures 2.6" tall, was produced in the late 40s to early 50s, and has an approximate value of $20-25.

Miniature Mallard drake, duckling, and hen, as decorated by Pat and designed by Helen. This family was only produced in the early 50s. The drake measures 2.5" tall, the duckling 1.2", and the hen 1.75" tall. Their approximate values are $15-18 for the adults and $4-6 for the duckling.

First the piece would go to the spray department before coming to be decorated. They were just masters at bringing out the shading in the body in the spraying department. Ann Baker was in charge there. Then they would come from the spray department on a hard surface, and we'd just touch them and there was our fingerprints. That was one of the hardest things I ever had to deal with. And the climbing cat, in order to grab it to paint it, its right up both sides of the body and it's horrible. There's nothing to grab. Actually, after you'd started a while, your fingers would get powdery, in the spray, and you were OK then.

We didn't do any dot eyes. That was in the miniatures. We had two-tone eyes with a white dot. Then there was brown and black. Then you went around the eye with a liner. And around the mouth. And that's all that was done with decorating, except for a blaze, of course, if they had one. And sometimes there was a nostril, too. I was asked to decorate the miniature Mama Skunk how I'd like to see it done, but they didn't choose it for the final production run. The tail style I painted was a lot more complicated. I also designed the Designers' Workshop Mama Zebra's face. That's one of my favorite animals. The one I have is from while we were still painting and

changing it, and it didn't have any design on it to follow yet. The ones that followed, that were designed for production, had the design imprinted on the zebra itself to expedite more zebras out the door. I'm real proud of that one...I think I've got my initials on the bottom. I also like the City and Country Mice. You wouldn't believe the detail! The Papa has a double man's monocle and oh lordy, those tails went out and around. Even the one I've got I couldn't keep the tail from breaking off at the end.

Bill Nicely and my husband Dick were high school chums. Bill asked me to go to a party to welcome a fellow home from the service. My husband was at that party, June 25, 1953. We've been married since 1954. I worked at Hagen-Renaker until September, 1956, and left when I was pregnant with my second child. I found I couldn't handle family and job, so I 'passed the torch' to a gal named Penny Leiber. It was a sad day for me. Some beautiful Designers' Workshop pieces came out of the company during that period. I loved it all! I just thought we were doing such a beautiful thing. There were 6 or 7 colors on the City and Country Mice, and that's where you get into a lot of expense. We painted each color, put the dots on, and the crosses on the baskets. We put the spots on the Dalmatian

This is Pat's version of how Maxine Renaker's Papa skunk should look, which is a bit different from the factory production run.

Mama and baby Designers' Workshop zebras. Stripe detail on these is a little different from the final factory production style. Designed by Helen Perrin Farnlund, the mama stands 5.5" tall and the baby 3.75" tall. Their approximate values are $140-150 for the mama and $75-80 for the baby.

The city mouse family, designed by Helen Perrin Farnlund, was produced in the early 50s, then again in the 60s and 80s with less elaborate decoration. Papa is 3.25" tall, baby is 2" tall, and Mama is 3" tall. Their approximate values are $40-50 for the adults and $20-30 for the little girl.

The country mouse family, designed by Helen Perrin Farnlund, was produced in the early 50s, then again in the 60s and 80s with less elaborate decoration. Papa measures 3.1" tall, baby 1.75" tall, and Mama is 3" tall. Their approximate values are $40-50 for the adults and $20-30 for the little boy. This set was frequently copied by foreign companies, with fairly good detail. One way to spot a copy is by looking at the ears, as the Hagen-Renaker mouse ears are much thinner and fragile than the thicker ones made by the competition.

dogs. I have a chipmunk, about 5" long, and we had to put on white marks, then went back and put hair marks all over the back, face, and feet. The TIME that is involved. Even in the miniatures, like with the Mallard family. You wonder how they could even make her, she took so much time! When I saw what Japan and other people have done, I really want to stick up for Design-

ers' Workshop and really come forward and say HEY you haven't seen what WE do!

Oh, you don't know the beautiful memories I have of working there! It just was so delightful. Everyone! I honestly can tell you they were some of the greatest years of my life, and I still dream I'm at the pottery after all these years.

Pat had written to Gayle Roller when the first *Hagen-Renaker Handbook* came out, to let Gayle know how excited she was about having worked there in the early years. Pat was delighted to be contacted for this book. It seems fitting that Pat has finally been able to tell her story, and that the fans of her decorating work have been able to meet the person whose artistry and decorating skills help bring the early Hagen-Renaker pieces to life!

14

Bill Nicely

Bill Nicely is not a familiar name to most Hagen-Renaker collectors, but he is certainly one of the main reasons that the company has managed to stay around as long as it has. Bill possesses just the right blend of technical know-how and appreciation for the art to provide vital support for the entire operation and guidance when troubleshooting problems.

Bill explains, "I started working there in March of 1948. I started in just as a regular after school worker. We were all very close in those early years. John and Maxine were almost like my mother and father. They are about 20 years my seniors. When I went to work for them I was only 16 years old. I was shorter than Maxine, and Maxine's pretty small. I was under 5-foot, and I weighed under 100 pounds. Now I'm 6'3", and I weigh a lot more than that, so I really grew up there. Maxine and I used to load kilns together, and I had to build myself a box to stand on so I could reach into the bottom of the kiln."

John Renaker recalls "In those days Maxine did almost all the hiring. Bill evidently heard there was work available. His stepmother worked for H-R and he probably learned about us from her. I do know that he grew about a foot in his first year. He used to load pottery in the top-loader kilns we had then, and had to swing on his stomach over the edge of the kiln in order to load shelves in the bottom. Before long he could reach it. He was very quick to learn and Maxine soon had him picking out orders, which he could do faster than anyone else. He met Cil, his future wife, in the early 50s, when she was working for us as a decorator."

Bill continues, "I eventually worked in all of the departments. After I'd been there a couple of years, John and Maxine went on a vacation trip to the beach for a week and left me in charge. Then after that, a couple of years later, we started Designers' Workshop. By that time, I was pretty familiar with all the departments and I was left to run that portion of it."

Bill Nicely dumping clay powder into a mixing vat that contains water.

One day Bill spotted this hippo in Maureen Love's work wastebasket. He seized it, claimed it for his own, and proudly displays it to this day.

These numbers written on the bottom of test pieces help the crew develop the proper colors.

"At that time we had about 15 buildings scattered around Monrovia; several of them were in miniatures. Then we built a rather large building, it was about a 40,000 square foot building, and moved everything into it. That was about 1957. In the early 60s, business became so bad that we sold that building and moved back into one of our original Quonset huts that we had started in. At that time we were down to no employees. We sent out a mailing, got some more orders in, and I started hiring back in this Quonset hut."

"But in the meantime, John had started the nursery business, so we had other facilities, in the form of nursery stock, land and that kind of thing. That included the San Dimas property by that time. When the pottery business started to pick up in Monrovia, in the old Quonset hut, we thought that it would be a good idea to move the pottery business to San Dimas and start making pottery there. So we did that. We moved everything and built a building in San Dimas, one of the buildings that we're still in. Business became good again, and we just kept growing and growing and growing, to the present day. At that time I was running the whole plant, I was doing everything. John was primarily concerned with the nursery business. In 1978, after 30-some years, I just got tired, and quit. I was off for 10 years. Then in 1988, Sue, and John and Maxine asked me to come back as a consultant, and that's what I've been doing. I work three half-days a week, or more if I'm needed. I do primarily technical consulting, maintenance, and all kinds of things to get the little things out of Sue's hair. Sue runs the plant now, quite well, and makes all of the major decisions. John and Maxine are retired from the business."

Bill can be described as the troubleshooter for the company. He has been involved in many key stages and aspects of its growth and development. For example, when the salesman for Florida was not responding to the requests of Disney World, Bill flew to Florida, fired the salesman and did a lot of work to get them set up to sell Hagen-Renaker. It was also Bill Nicely and Jim Renaker that fired George Good, who was their national sales manager for some years, and then Bill proceeded to set up new salesmen throughout the California region. And when the company reached the rocky period of the early 1960's, Bill put together mailings that brought in business and got things going again.

Nell Bortells recalls working closely with Bill at Designers' Workshop. She said "When I wanted to create different colors, he'd have to figure out from, I'd say like oh 2% of this particular brown and 1% of that and so forth. Then he'd try to work out a formula from what I would say, since many of the colors used were not available ready-made. Bill determined which tints or pigments—and how much of each—were needed to arrive at the formula for mixing the desired colors and shades, both for the slip tints and the decoration paints. Also, he has great knowledge and expertise with glaze."

Bill continues, "Sometimes a piece would go with one decoration on it, and then for various reasons in mid-stream change it entirely. Sometimes it was a technical reason. For example, during the 50s when the Korean War started, we were hit pretty hard because some of the colors we were using were put on a restricted list. Cobalt's were very difficult colors, so we had to do a lot of shuffling around to match colors. Not all of them were successful, so we just would go from a brown to a dun or whatever would work." For a while the company used a water-based paint pigment called Aurasperse® to get the colors needed, but that rubbed off and wasn't used for very long. "The other thing is that when we're making something, we might try 50 or 100 different things. You might find animals around with numbers and letters written on them. That would be color tests that we were running, or decoration tests that we were running. We still do that, in fact."

As far as having creative input, Bill recalls "I had a few original designs of my own. One that comes to mind was the half duck. Tom Masterson did that one. He had the mama duck and the baby duck. They were talking about putting it on a pond, and wondered what would fit in with it. I told them I thought a half duck would do well. At first they didn't understand what I meant. You know what the girls around the plant called that for years? Duck butt! They made duck butts!"

Over his long association with Hagen-Renaker, Bill's devotion to the company and his untiring dedication to the operation and its people helped keep it alive, whether it involved technical matters, sales, or personnel. He recently summed up his approach when discussing the difficulty sometimes encountered in making the mold for some pieces. He strongly believes that you "don't want to restrict the artist or hamper the creative process." Once the piece is created, then the technical people can work with the artist to make the piece suitable for molding. Sometimes, just moving a part 0.1" will make the mold come out OK, but you "always do it after the fact, never before." Bill's meticulous attention to detail has also served well in this telling of the history of the Hagen-Renaker company. Thank you, Bill!

The adorable little "duck butt" measures .5" tall, the mama duck 1.25" tall, and the duck pond 3.8" by 2.5". All were designed by Tom Masterson, and ran for several years from the mid-50s to the 90s. The mama duck in a Mallard decoration is worth $12-15, otherwise the two ducks are worth approximately $2-4 each, and the pond is worth approximately $4-5.

15

Robyn Sikking

There were several designers that worked part-time or free-lanced for Hagen-Renaker. Robyn Sikking was one of those designers. She and her husband Bruce Lytton Sikking had their own ceramic company, Robyn's Ceramics.

Robyn explains, "We started it during the war—1940s, and continued on until the 1970s. My husband died in 1974, and I continued for several years. It was located in Fallbrook, California, and also in Idyllwild, California. The first years we specialized in Christmas ceramics and angels—all kinds of figurines. After we were copied so much and so fast we changed to the rustic animals and St. Francis—Swan Girl and Fishing Boy and such as that."

Seated St. Francis and his animal friends.

Three rustic donkeys done for Robyn's Ceramics. Note the similar finish as was used on the squirrels made for Hagen-Renaker.

Robyn Sikking in a photo taken from her Robyn's Ceramics catalog.

Swan Girl and her feathered friends.

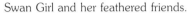

Robyn originally designed Star Babies for Hagen-Renaker, but they were moved over to Walker-Renaker since they were produced in porcelain. Standing 5" tall, each Star Baby represents a zodiac sign. Pictured are Taurus, Gemini, and Scorpio. Approximate value is $15-20.

"I worked for Hagen-Renaker part time, as I had my own work to do also. I designed a line of Star Babies for Hagen-Renaker. I don't know if they were ever in the line. Also quite a few salt and pepper shakers. I did some of the squirrels for Hagen-Renaker, both large and in the miniatures. I have many more in my own lines and I reserved the right to make all of my squirrels including the miniatures, medium size and life size. I had input on the finish. I think we made the first mold and I finished and decorated it. I know we did on the Star Babies."

According to the sales catalog for Robyn's Ceramics, "Every member of the Angel Family is an original design created by Robyn. Each figurine has its name inscribed on the bottom in gold. It is also marked, 'Original Design by Robyn'." The catalog goes on to describe the process of making the figurines, including some pieces that were so complicated that they took as many as seven sections of mold to complete. Each item followed a process that involved four trips through the kiln, and the last step consisted of applying the 22 karat gold trim before the final firing.

As an interesting side note, the catalog refers to "one of the most painstaking tasks of all—the painting of the little faces so that each angel has just the right expression and is as perfect in detail as possible, and this requires much skill." One of the face painters was Robyn's daughter, Laurilyn Burson, who later went on to work in other ceramics and eventually for Hagen-Renaker.

This is the sticker on the underside of the Scorpio Star Baby.

Three members of the Chatter family are shown here. Mr. Chatter stands 3.8" tall, Mrs. Chatter is 4" tall, and baby Chat is 2.5" tall. Missing are babies Chit, Chew, and Chunk. They were produced in the mid-50s and have an approximate value of $30-35 for the adults and $20-25 for the babies.

16

Laurilyn Burson

Laurilyn Burson was one of the more recently hired employees at Hagen-Renaker. She is a native of California, and earned her bachelors degree in art from San Diego State University. She also worked for Hagen-Renaker briefly, between colleges, while her mother was a designer there. She explains, "I worked for my parents 'painting faces' until I left for college. After college I made my mother's squirrels and developed my own line of ceramics while raising four children. We moved to Oroco, Maine for my former husband to get his doctorate. I made pottery to keep the family afloat. It was my only 'claim to fame.' Craft shows were just starting and my work was well received."

One interesting area that Laurilyn dabbled in, and became quite proficient at, was the craft of Raku. She was featured, as Laurilyn Allin, in an article in *Popular Handicraft & Hobbies* magazine, in their June-July 1973 issue, demonstrating this unusual process. Briefly, when a ceramic piece goes into the kiln for its last firing, it is removed while it is red hot and the glaze has melted. Using tongs, the piece is quickly put into a covered container with leaves or anything combustible. It will want to burn, but because it cannot get oxygen from the room it pulls it out of the clay and glaze and causes them to reduce. This causes changes in the glaze, sometimes turning them an iridescent red or vibrant turquoise or luster gold, and the clay turns a soft charcoal. The piece is then immersed into a container of cold water where the colors are fixed. She would demonstrate this process at craft shows and fascinate the crowds. It was an exciting process because each piece came out unique and could not be reproduced.

Later, when she returned to California, she continues "I designed for a company in San Diego called 'Clay in Mind,' then hired on in 1979 at Freeman-McFarlin (in San Marcos) because I wanted to learn more about mold making. I worked with Rich Steckman making molds, blocks, and cases. I told the Renakers when Freeman-McFarlin was for sale, and they bought it in 1980. They

kept me on. A few years later, after they sold the San Marcos plant, Rich and I were moved to Encinitas. I worked with John Renaker to develop the new pieces that Helen and Maureen designed. I did research and development with John Renaker, and later Maxine, in Encinitas. It was my favorite time. I admire John Renaker. His insights, business savvy, and personableness are fabulous. And Maxine would come every morning and we prayed for the company."

"Regarding development of the Collectors' Series of pieces, Joan Berkwitz and Kathleen Rose asked me to decorate some bisque pieces they had. In talking with them I realized that there was a need for collector's horses. Maureen and I discussed doing it on our own or through the company. We both preferred 'staying in company,' so to speak. Sue was agreeable. John and Maxine were very lenient with me. I had been given permission to take some of the work to my home, as my husband is not well." That was how "Jamboree" and "Encore" were done. Laurilyn left Hagen-Renaker soon after that.

Maureen and Laurilyn have since teamed up to form the ceramics company "Made With Love," and have created two horses to date. The "Wild Horse," originally issued in black and then in several one-of-a-kind colors has been an interesting and beautiful model. The Clydesdale, issued in both matte and gloss finish, is the current piece. The next piece, according to Maureen, might be the black necked stilt, a black and white bird with long pink legs. She says that "Laurilyn would rather do birds than horses. She's real good about decorating them. Laurilyn is a great person. We're great friends."

When asked what her favorite artist of all time is, Laurilyn responds "I like Rembrandt for his use of light and realism, yet I love some of the primitive type sculpture for its simplicity and whimsy. I admire innovative art, but not modern." This mix of tastes has certainly served Laurilyn well over her long and varied career in art.

Laurilyn demonstrating the craft of Raku.

This Clydesdale model was produced in matte and glossy bay. It was also made in a variety of custom colors, including this dapple gray. It stands 5.5" tall, was designed by Maureen Love in the 90s, and decorated by Laurilyn Burson. Approximate value is $150-180.

Wild horse was designed by Maureen Love and decorated by Laurilyn Burson. It stands 6.5" tall and was produced in matte black, and several custom colors such as this splashy pinto. Produced in the 90s, it has an approximate value of $120-150.

—17—

Other Key People

So many more people were involved with the Hagen-Renaker Company that it is impossible to name them all. However, there are several key individuals that will be remembered here.

Will Climes

According to Bill Nicely, "Will Climes was a designer, who had worked at potteries for many years before he came in with us. He had his own designing company, and he was a good designer. He was a very nice man, too. He helped us with a lot of the experimental work that we had done. He made a lot of the rock plaques for us. He was a good technical designer. He did ashtrays and bowls, and that kind of thing very well. Another thing that Will did was a robin that we used to make. It was about as big as a man's fist, and with a pink breast. That idea and design pretty much came from when Will worked at the Wrigley Pottery on Catalina Island."

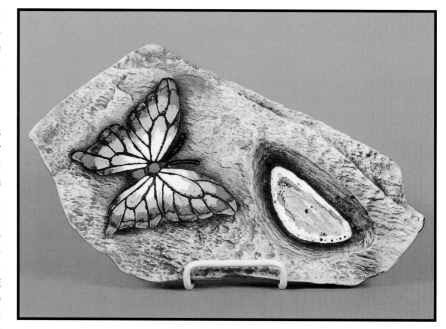

This butterfly tray made of the same material as the rock plaques measures 12" long. It was produced in the late 50s to early 60s and is considered rare.

This stunning snapper was designed by Will Climes. Other fish featured on these plaques include barracuda, perch, pompano, and corbina. All of the rock plaques were made in the late 50s, and are considered rare.

Will Climes, taken in 1959.

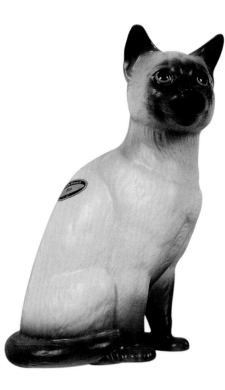

Dick the sitting Siamese cat was produced in the early 60s. He is 6.5" tall and has an approximate value of $70-75.

If this robin looks familiar, it is because it is one of the most-copied items that Hagen-Renaker made. The irony is that it may not even be an original design for the company, but one that they obtained from another. This robin was made intermittently from the 50s through the 80s, stands 3.1" tall, and has an approximate value of $25-35.

Harry the lying Siamese cat measures 4.8" tall, was produced in the early 60s, and has an approximate value of $70-75.

Helen Perrin Farnlund talks of Will as "a really good designer, and a nice guy. He had nice ware. It's kinda too bad that it didn't succeed. Will started to work at Hagen-Renaker because his pottery went belly-up. His pottery failed before Hagen-Renaker had troubles."

Jim Renaker recalls Will as a kind, patient man who was very helpful in teaching others about mold making, including Martha Armstrong Hand. Jim remembers Will as "a very patient man and a self-taught mold maker. He once showed me his very first mold. He managed to get a little figure of a dachshund that had its legs welded together, as if standing in a sack. It had taken him 13 pieces to make a mold of that. He kept it all those years, I guess as a momento," Jim laughingly remembers. "He was a master potter and a great mold maker. Will worked on the big plaques; that was one of his projects. The ones that look like fossils, with fish and so forth. Will took a great delight in all sorts of things, and was always good for a joke and a laugh."

Tom the walking Siamese cat was produced in the early 60s. He is part of a set with comrades Dick and Harry. Tom stands 5.75" tall and has an approximate value of $70-75.

Bill's favorite story about Will was that "he had this Porsche and he was always bragging about his Porsche. He parked it out in front of the mold shop one day, and I went out and got a piece of cardboard and cut what looked like the stub of a key. I stuck it down in the louvers in the back, so it looked like you had to wind it up to get it going. But he was somebody that you could do that to. Will just laughed it off."

Will died of a heart attack while working for Hagen-Renaker. Jim comments "He was a reed-thin man, but had a bad heart. He died young." Will Climes died in 1960.

Bill Mintzer and Joe Griffith

According to Jim, "The guy who headed up the mold shop was Bill Mintzer. Bill was a navy man, in the navy as a corpsman during the war, and he spent quite a bit of time on Iwo Jima. Pretty well decorated sailor. The other guy that was his contemporary was Joe Griffith. Joe had been a tank driver in the army. These were the guys that basically ran the mold shop." While Pat O'Brien Kristof had a lot of respect for them, she didn't feel close to them because they "were always 'scatting' around, here, there, and everywhere and never had time to stop and chat. They were very busy in what they were doing."

The fellows who ran the mold shop. Left to Right: Benny Basset, Joe Griffith, and Bill Mintzer. This photo was taken in late 1959.

Nell Bortells recalls Bill and Joe were "two of the nicest guys." When Hagen-Renaker was beginning to run into problems, "they apparently could see the writing on the wall. They tried to start a business and then tried to help us designers get started. This was McAfee, a pottery that already existed; in fact it was right across from one of our old potteries." Sadly, Bill and Joe were killed in a car accident on the freeway. "They were on the freeway, and a woman on one of the top ramps went off and landed on them. I was on jury duty, locked up in Los Angeles, for the Sirhan Sirhan trial at the time (1969). I didn't learn about that until months later when I was finally off the trial. And that was a very sad thing. They had been with the pottery for years, going way back to the beginning."

Ruth and Rich Steckman

Ruth Steckman started working for McFarlin Pottery (later Freeman-McFarlin) as a finisher in 1945 in their El Monte plant. From there, she moved around to glazes, loading kilns, and eventually the mold department. Four of her six children worked at least briefly in the pottery business, but only her son Rich made a career of it. He trained in the mold shop of the El Monte plant under Ernie Flores. When the San Marcos plant was started around 1970, Rich was transferred there to start the mold shop. He eventually became their head mold maker. International Multifoods purchased Freeman-McFarlin in 1972, and Maynard Freeman's son Rick ran the San Marcos plant. Ruth was transferred to San Marcos in 1974 by the new owners, and started the warehouse. She helped in every area of the plant except decorating.

When Hagen-Renaker bought the plant from International Multifoods, everyone was let go. But Hagen-Renaker hired back a few of the employees, plus added some of their own people from the San Dimas plant. As Jim Renaker explains, "Rich and Ruth Steckman were at the top of the list! When we took over the pottery business in San Marcos, we got Rich with it. I was to go back and take part in that. I was to be a teacher of mold making. I found right off the bat that I couldn't teach Rich anything...he already had it down pat. He was one of the best mold makers I ever saw in my life."

Ruth worked for the San Marcos plant for three years, then retired. Her total career in pottery covered 38 years and she "enjoyed all of it. Rich worked there until they closed the plant, then he started a mold shop in his garage." At age 77, Ruth enjoys retirement, and spending time with her children.

George Good

According to William Wiemhoff, per his interview with Maxine Renaker, "George Good joined the Hagen-Renaker operation as sales representative in 1948. He had a lot of ideas and suggestions related to sales, *i.e.*, displayers, etc. It was also he who originally suggested that Hagen-Renaker obtain a license from Walt Disney to produce ceramics of Disney characters."

Bill Nicely explains that "George Good was our national sales manager for some years. He had a major sales company that covered the entire United States, and he had many, many lines. And he did a lot of things in Japan after that time. He had his own company, Good and Company, and he represented us entirely, and at one time he represented us for the whole country. George also represented Josef Originals, and he was instrumental in taking them to Japan."

This photo was taken at Ruth Steckman's 1983 retirement party. She is seated next to John Renaker (wearing the hat) and her son Rich Steckman is standing between them.

This impish mouse was produced by Josef Originals. The card reads "George Good/California/Josef Originals." He measures 1.75" tall and has an approximate value of $8-10.

This adorable duck was made in the Freeman-McFarlin plant. Measuring 4.5" tall, it later was also produced in white or gold. It has an approximate value of $8-10.

This little deer came attached to this card. It measures 1.25" tall, and has an approximate value of $6-8. There were several other animals in this series, including a cow, bull, horses, and rabbits. All had this sort of water color appearance to their glaze.

Mary Renaker adds, "Dad began studying Berlitz Japanese with Noboru ("Nobe") Inamoto, a teacher at USC, because George was so insistent that they take the line to Japan and have it made there—cheap imports were the wave of the future. Dad figured he would have to learn the language in order to do business there, and we were immersed in Japanese gardens, food, sake cups, calligraphy, Kabuki theater and movies for a while—it was actually really great! But then Dad decided he didn't want to take the line to Japan and lose control of its manufacture (that would take all the fun out of it). George took his samples and had them copied over there. He was fired, took his sales force with him and most of the accounts, too."

Bill continues, "Jim and I fired George. But then we didn't have any other irons in the fire. I started reaching out for all the irons I could remember, and Phil Leitsch was one of them. Phil was one of four salesmen working for Good and Company in California, working the Southern California area along with Don Mitchell. He had been fired by George just before we fired George. I called Phil right away, and he came back and became the California salesman and he did a remarkable job. He was my mainstay at that period of time. He was a great guy. He also helped bail us out on some trouble we had with Disney World."

David Renaker

Mary Renaker explains about her older brother David, "Sue has a twin brother David who got his Ph.D. from Harvard before he was 27. He already had a wife and daughter and took a job teaching English Literature at San Francisco State in 1968 and has been there ever since." Prior to that, according to Nell Bortells, "David did the illustrations for the 'Little Horribles;' they made little cards to go in the plastic boxes with them. He also generally came up with the names for them. He used to come down and do illustrations for the sales sheets, too." Mary concludes that, "He has no interest whatsoever in Hagen-Renaker, and neither do his kids." The Renaker family bought out his shares in the company years ago.

Moss Renaker

Nell Bortells fondly recalls her association with Moss Renaker. "She is John's mother. I met her because I worked one summer at Walker Pottery when I was going to high school, and she was in charge of decorating. Moss was a funny, fun person. She was very witty, and I admired her wit. You know, it's just kind of fun to sit there as a kid and listen to grown-ups talk. I worked there that one summer. Then she started what I believe they called the 'Putti Factory.' It was these little pink, bisque angels. She also did animals with flowers and things on them. It was across the street from where Walker Pottery was." Putti means angels or cherubs, and the factory was Walker-Renaker. John Renaker was also involved in starting this venture.

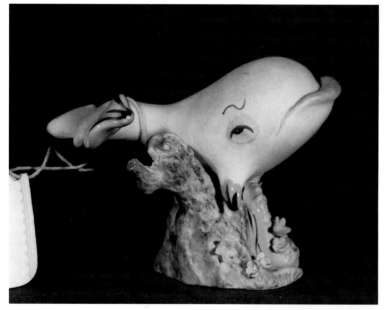

This whale was one of the porcelain bisque figurines produced at Walker-Renaker Pottery. The attached tag says "copyright 1954," and also has the following poem. "The whale is much too large, it seems/To navigate in little streams/He's fond of moving to and fro/And that takes lots of H2O." He is 2.5" tall, and has an approximate value $35-40.

This series of pink porcelain animals was produced at the Walker-Renaker Pottery. Their names are Forget-Me-Not, Pig O' My Heart, Horse of a Different Color, and Cock of the Walk. Measuring about 3" tall, they each have an approximate value of $15-18. There were other animals in the series, and there are also many copies of these animals.

Mary Renaker explains that, "Moss is a botanical name like Daisy, Rose, Iris or Fern. Granny Moss said she used to shock her fellow workers at Walker-Renaker Pottery by jumping up on her chair and yelling 'Hooray for Roosevelt!' which horrified all the dignified Republican ladies."

And of course, it was Moss, who worked at Walker Pottery during World War II that suggested to John that he go into the pottery business, eventually giving rise to the Hagen-Renaker Pottery company!

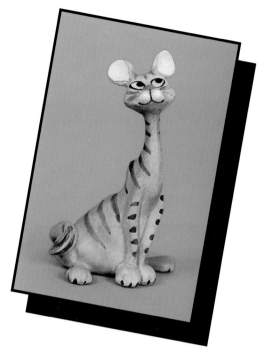

Moss Renaker wrote a series of poems about animals for *Successful Farming* magazine, and also published them in a book called *Zany Zoo.* Each poem was accompanied by an illustration, and Tom Masterson and Nell Bortells designed animals based on those drawings. This lion measures 3" tall. All of the Zany Zoo animals are considered rare.

This cat from the Zany Zoo measures 3.75" tall. They were produced by Hagen-Renaker for a short time in the early 60s and were accompanied with a studio card describing the piece. All of the Zany Zoo animals are considered rare.

Moss Renaker designed this Calico Cat, which is the companion piece to the Gingham Dog designed by John Renaker. It measures 2.6" tall, was produced in the late 40s, and is considered rare.

Don Winton

There were several designers who only worked part time for Hagen-Renaker. During the late 1950s, Don Winton briefly shared his expertise with the company. He had his own company, Twin Winton, that was well established, but when they fell on some hard times, according to Bill Nicely, Don created many of the Disney pieces for Hagen-Renaker. He also made a few other note-worthy animals, including a model of "Butch," the Cocker Spaniel which was owned by illustrator Albert Staehle and appeared on covers of *The Saturday Evening Post.*

Flower the lovable skunk from the movie *Bambi* was produced in the late 50s. He stands 2.25" tall, and has an approximate value of $175-200.

Dumbo the flying elephant was made in the late 50s. He measures 5.75" tall and has an approximate value of $250-300.

This is the Designers' Workshop version of Bambi, standing 3.5" tall. He was produced in the late 50s, and has an approximate value of $275-300.

Nana the motherly dog from *Peter Pan* keeps an eye on young Michael. Nana measures 1.5" tall and Michael is 1.1" tall. Both were produced in the late 50s. Nana has an approximate value of $120-135 and Michael $130-150.

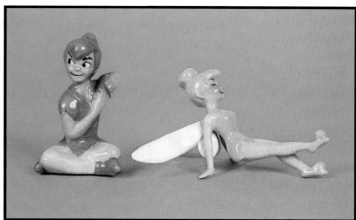

Peter Pan and companion Tinker Bell were produced in the late 50s. Peter is 1.75" tall and Tinker Bell (intended to be a shelf-sitter) is 1.4" tall. The approximate value for Peter Pan is $120-130 and for Tinkerbell $350-400. She was also issued in a kneeling and flying pose.

This 5.5" figure of Lady from the movie *Lady and the Tramp* is actually a bank. She was produced in the late 50s and has an approximate value of $300-350.

This handy looking figure was called Practical Pig. This version is a bank, and he stands 7" tall. Produced in the late 50s, his approximate value is $300-350. Any other colors on this mold would not be the Disney version, and would be worth less.

This bank version of Figaro the cat measures 5.5" tall. It was produced in the late 50s and has an approximate value of $250-300.

Butch the Cocker Spaniel was designed by Don Winton after the dog owned by illustrator Albert Staehle. The live Butch was familiar to Americans due to his appearances on the cover of *The Saturday Evening Post* in the 40s. This Designers' Workshop model measures 5.25" tall, was produced in the late 50s, and has an approximate value of $45-55.

This buff Cocker Spaniel was made from the same mold that turned out the Butch Cocker Spaniel. This buff version was made in the late 60s and is considered rare.

Silver the Persian cat came in two sizes, this one being the smaller of the two at 9.5". The larger Silver measures 12.25". Both were produced in the 50s and 60s, and the larger one was also produced in the 80s. The smaller one (shown) has an approximate value of $50-55, and the larger one is worth $60-65.

This tortoise came in brown, and in green with a gold shell (shown). He was made in the 50s, and again in the 70s, and his approximate value is $10-12 for brown and $20-25 for green with gold.

Quentin and Agnes Japs

It certainly took the men and women in the trenches, the sales force, to keep the product in front of the buyers. An example of that group is Quentin and Agnes Japs. Married in 1946, they were on their honeymoon in California, waiting to return to Minnesota to open a resort. A friend suggested that they meet John Renaker and look into the pottery business. Quent became Hagen-Renaker's first salesman, and covered seven states in the midwest. Agnes helped out at the large gift shows in Chicago, Milwaukee, and the permanent showroom in Minneapolis. Business became so good that Quent hired four more salesmen. The orders were so plentiful that they were forced to take leave from November till January while the factory caught up. He recalls that the hottest selling item was the "Holy Cow." Quent observes that eventually the foreign competition moved in, and the orders fell off. Then the stores wondered why their sales faltered. It was because the foreign product did not match the quality of Hagen-Renaker. At age fifty, Quent moved on to another job because he was getting tired of life on the road. He proudly recalls that he was the only salesman that the Dayton Company would allow to deliver goods without prior authorization, because they knew the quality of what they would be getting and the reliability of the service. Pride like that, at all levels, helped to keep the company strong.

Madame Fluff the Persian cat was designed in the mid-50s by Armae Conacher. Armae worked for Hagen-Renaker briefly in the 50s, doing illustrations for the order forms, and other art work. While she designed several pieces, these two were the only ones that translated well for production in ceramic. Armae went on to design for George Good and made a doll line (Good Lil' Kiddies) and a line of Easter bunnies. She is currently making porcelain dolls that she describes as dolls that "are not just sitting, looking straight ahead with no apparent reason for being." She recently had one accepted by the Home Shopping Network. Madam Fluff measures 5" tall, was only produced in this tan color, and has an approximate value of $100-120.

The original Holy Cow is pictured in chapter 3, but this is a more recent creation also bearing the name Holy Cow. She was designed by Nell Bortells, stands 2.5" tall, and was produced in the mid-80s. Her approximate value is $13-15.

Puff is the kitten of Madam Fluff and was designed by Armae. She was produced in the mid-50s, stands 2.5" tall, and has an approximate value of $80-100.

Disney artists Russell Schroeder and Perry Russ designed several pieces for Hagen-Renaker in the early 80s for the *Fantasia* series. Pictured here from that movie is Mickey Mouse as the Sorcerer's Apprentice. Along with him is the magical broom. Both Mickey and the broom stand 2.6" tall, and have approximate values of $150-180. Next to them is the tiny *Fantasia* mushroom Hop Low. It measures .75" tall, and has an approximate value of $35-40.

Madama Upanova was designed by Russell Schroeder and Perry Russ. She is 3.25" tall, was produced in the early 80s, and has an approximate value of $175-200.

18

The Name Game

One of the unique and endearing characteristics of the Designers' Workshop Hagen-Renaker animals is that most of them were given names. How those names were assigned varied with the piece, some having colorful histories and some being named after personal pets. Bill Nicely admits that it was his least favorite part of the job, yet Jim Renaker enjoyed it. In fact, several of the names originated, according to Bill, while having a beer after work with Jim, Will Climes, and occasionally John Renaker, and Tom Masterson at the local watering hole. According to Bill, it got pretty riotous at times, but they did get some of the names out of it. Bill concedes that "the pieces that were the toughest to name were the cats. We tried to give the Siamese cats Siamese names, but I don't think we were very successful. Rabbits were easy to do, with Flopsy, Mopsy, and that kind of thing. The more obscure animals, the ducks, the chickens, with names like Alex and Elizabeth, those were names that just went through my mind and basically that was the way those things were named. There is some duplication in the names, like the duplicate Tabby cats, we'd forgotten what we had named them. We were pretty desperate at one point for names. It doesn't seem like a big thing, but it is after you have so many names to come up with."

Alex the rooster came in white (shown) and reddish brown. He stands 6.75" tall and was made intermittently from the 50s through the 80s. He was designed by Maureen Love and his approximate value is $30-45.

Little bunnies (left to right) Flopsy, Mopsy, and Cottontail were all designed by Helen Perrin Farnlund in the mid-50s. They were produced in this brown color and in white. Flopsy measures 1.5" tall, and the other two are 2.5" tall. Their approximate values are $35-40 each.

Elizabeth the hen was designed by Maureen Love, and was produced in white and reddish brown (shown). She measures 4.25" tall, and was produced intermittently from the 50s through the 80s. Her approximate value is $30-45.

This is one of the cats who bears the name Tabby on an oval Hagen-Renaker sticker. It measures 4.75" tall, was produced in the late 50s and early 80s, and has an approximate value of $40-50. This mold also came in gray, orange, and calico.

Bill further explains, "Tom Masterson, who did the majority of the dogs, worked best from live models. So, the figurine often bore the name of the dog it was modeled from. For instance, the Dachshund he did was John Renaker's dog, and its name was Beanbag. Beanbag was introduced to another designer's dog, Will Climes's dog, and they had six pups. We designed all six of them, and named them what the owners named them. One of them was named Tiger, which was my dog, and there's one of those sitting at my feet right now, my third Tiger. She's fourteen years old. Some of the names, the girls had pet names for the pieces that they were doing in the

Winston the English Bulldog stands 3.5" tall and was produced in the 50s and 60s. He was designed by Tom Masterson, came with varying amounts of shading, and has an approximate value of $60-65.

Beanbag the overworked mother Dachshund is accompanied here with her puppies, starting from the left, Henessy, Tiger, Elsa, Lenk, and Dutch. Kutchen is missing from this photo. The puppies all measure 1.25-1.5" tall except for Lenk who is .5" tall. Beanbag is 2" tall. They were all designed by Tom Masterson, were produced in various shades of brown or tan, and have approximate values of $40-45. The basket was also designed by Tom Masterson, measures 2.75" long, and has an approximate value of $40-50. All of these items were made in the 50s and 60s.

departments. As long as they were good names, we used those."

An unusual inspiration was used for naming the Bulldog Winston. It was an easy connection for those assigning names to associate the stern Bulldog with the then current Prime Minister of Great Britain, Sir Winston Churchill.

Five famous Thoroughbreds, Man O' War, Terrang, Swaps, Silky Sullivan, and Kelso provided names for five of the Designers' Workshop horses, as well as the parallel miniatures. Maureen Love loved to visit the Santa Anita race track and spent hours studying the horses there. But another equine sculpture was also inspired by her sessions at the track; the awesome Belgian mare Sespe Violette. This mare was part of the team of mighty Belgians that was used to pull the starting gate. Maureen was quite taken by the strength and beauty of these animals.

Top left: Man O' War the Thoroughbred race horse stands 7" tall and was designed by Maureen Love. Produced in the 60s and 70s, he has an approximate value of $125-175.

Center left: Terrang the Thoroughbred race horse stands 6.25" tall and was produced in the 60s and 70s. He was designed by Maureen Love and has an approximate value of $125-175.

Top right: Swaps the Thoroughbred race horse measures 6.75" tall and was designed by Maureen Love. He was produced in the 60s and 70s and has an approximate value of $125-175.

Center right: Silky Sullivan the Thoroughbred race horse is 6.5" tall and was produced in the 60s and 70s. Designed by Maureen Love, he has an approximate value of $125-175.

Bottom right: Kelso the Thoroughbred race horse is the only one of the five in a moving position. Measuring 6.5" tall, he was produced in the 60s and 70s, and was designed by Maureen Love. Due to his unusual position, his approximate value is $225-275.

Sespe Violette the Belgian mare stands 6" tall. This is the honey sorrel/palomino color she was produced in. She was also made in chestnut. She was produced in the 50s and 60s, designed by Maureen Love, and has an approximate value of $900-1000.

Sespe Violette the Belgian mare is shown here in chestnut. She was also made in a palomino/sorrel color. Produced in the 50s and 60s, her approximate value is $900-1000, with this chestnut color being the more rare color.

Another place where Maureen spent much time for inspiration was the ranch of friends Jimmie and Edna Nelson, in San Gabriel, California. The Nelsons raised Arabians, and Maureen sketched, and later modeled, many of their horses. At least two of the Hagen-Renaker Designers' Workshop Arabians bear the name of Nelson horses, the Arabians Ferseyn and Nataf. Abu Farwa was a local Arabian at the Kellogg Ranch in Southern California. The horses modeled after real horses usually bore the name of their live counter-part, and as much as possible, the coloring. Bill recalls that Maureen was good about giving the horse owners a copy of the sculpture of their horse, and of course they were pleased.

Abu Farwa the Arabian stallion was produced in the mid-50s. He stands 6" tall, and came only in white or white with gray shading. Designed by Maureen Love, he has an approximate value of $400-500, with the older, more detailed horses (see facial detail shown here) being worth more.

Sculptures of horses owned by Jimmie and Edna Nelson, Wagon Wheel Ranch, as designed by Maureen Love. Left to right: Ibn Nataf, Lanada, Skowranas, Ferseyn, Nataf, and Marranas. Ferseyn and Nataf became Hagen-Renaker horses.

One of the mysteries of the Designers' Workshop horses is the horse that collectors refer to as the "Love Appaloosa." That horse does not bear the name of its real life counter-part, an Appaloosa mare named OK Rain Dance. *Western Horseman Magazine* featured an article written by Maggie Kennedy, owner of OK Rain Dance, complete with photos taken by Maggie, of Maureen sketching her horse. According to Maggie, "OK was our ranch name for O'Shea, my maiden name, and Kennedy, my husband's name. This was my favorite Appaloosa mare, in life and in sculpture." Bill Nicely's best guess is that the horse figurine was not very popular and was not made for very long, hence it was not around long enough to be named.

Another Designers' Workshop horse, the Quarter Horse Two Bits was named by Jim Renaker, the punster of the family (two bits...a quarter...groan!). Jim took great pleasure in coming up with many of the "punny" names for the Little Horribles line. Nell Bortells would sculpt them, and Jim would name them. These included such playful names as Bag in a Sack, which described the old woman standing in a sack, and Hole in the Head, showing a man with a hole through his head and his hand, pointing an index finger through the hole. He also helped come up with some of the Walker-Renaker pink bisque animal names, including Bum Steer.

Maureen Love sketching at the OK Ranch. She is actually sketching the stallion OK Ya-Ta-Hey, who will serve as a model for the Appaloosa figurine representing OK Rain Dance.

Two Bits the Quarter Horse stallion came in buckskin (shown), dark bay, and a special run in palomino. He was produced intermittently throughout the 50s, 60s, 70s, and 80s, and stands 5.75" tall. He has an approximate value of $125-200, with the bay from the 80s being the least valuable.

Appaloosa horse who did not bear the name of its real-life model, the mare OK Rain Dance. This horse measures 4.75" tall, was produced in the 60s, and has an approximate value of $350-400. It came in two versions, with the spots carved into the horse's rump (as shown here) and with the rump smooth with spots painted on.

Hole in the Head and Bag in a Sack are two pieces from the Little Horribles line. Hole in the Head is 2.25" tall and Bag in a Sack is 2.5" tall. Both were made in the late 50s, designed by Nell Bortells, and have an approximate value of $50-60.

This Designers' Workshop dragon was made in limited quantities in the 80s. It measures 9" tall, was produced in green (shown) or in purple, and was designed by Helen Perrin Farnlund. It has an approximate value of $250-300.

Bum Steer was produced by Walker-Renaker in the mid-50s. It stands 2" tall, is made of porcelain, and has an approximate value of $15-18.

Close up view of the face of the Designers' Workshop dragon.

Jim also recalls how two other pieces came to be, at the San Marcos factory. "The game Dungeons and Dragons™ was popular during the San Marcos era (early 1980's). There were dragons everywhere in the culture, and most of them were depicted as monstrous things. My dad had the idea that we should make a baby dragon. It was a *tour de force* to get it through the mold shop. The wings, and mane were stuck on as separate pieces in the casting shop, and the gold detail required a third firing. We certainly didn't make a whole lot of them! Also, the cow was a good thing. My daughter was in Ag school at the time, and I had her get me a judging book, so that was done from the perfect Holstein cow, out of a judge's guide book."

When Maureen Love created Rajah the adult elephant, it was decided he needed a rider. Nell Bortells did some research and designed this elephant rider after the actor Sabu, who rode elephants in movies in the 40s. She got into a lengthy discussion with others at the company, trying to convince them that this indeed was the proper position for riding an elephant. Hagen-Renaker calls this rider Mahout.

Holstein Cow was made in the 80s with her calf. She measures 5" tall, came only in black and white, and was designed by Maureen Love. The approximate value is $70-80.

Skywalker the rearing horse stands 4.5" tall. Designed by Maureen Love, he is still available for a retail price of $16.

Recently, in 1997 and 1998, a series of horses were released in the specialty line, the models that are larger than the miniatures, but smaller than the old Designers' Workshop. Susan Nikas held a contest, via the internet, for people to submit name suggestions for the new horse models, and the winners were each awarded a test color model of the mold that they named. The winners were the Thoroughbred family of Mistweaver, Quicksilver, and Raindrop, the Morgan family of Shiloh, Liberty Belle, and Legacy, the Appaloosa family of Orion, Kamiah, and Sizzle, and the rearing stallion Skywalker. As Susan said in her closing paragraph of the message announcing the winners, "I want to thank you all for your thoughtful, creative entries. It was a difficult decision. I narrowed it down to three or four finalists in each category and then decided on winners from there. It was completely subjective and I thank all of you for your efforts. I think it is nice to go back to this old tradition of naming our pieces and with your help, I have done that."

Center right one: Thoroughbred specialty series family Quicksilver (mare), Mistweaver, (stallion), and Raindrop (foal). These horses were designed by Maureen Love, measure 3.1", 2.75", and 2.5" tall, and are still available at retail prices of $14 for the adults and $10 for the foal.

Center right two: Morgan specialty series family Shiloh (stallion), Legacy (foal) and Liberty Belle (mare). These horses were designed by Maureen Love, measure 3.1", 1.8", and 2.3" tall, and are still available at retail prices of

Bottom right: Appaloosa specialty series family Orion (stallion), Kamiah (mare), and Sizzle (foal). These horses were designed by Maureen Love, measure 3.1", 2.5", and 2.4" tall, and are still available at retail prices for $14 for the adults and $10 for the foal.

─19─

All Work and No Play...

The crew at Hagen-Renaker worked hard, and played hard, too. Here are a few examples of playful or humorous events, as told in the following stories:

Helen Perrin Farnlund: "At one time Maxine thought it would be fun to make molded candies—we could make much more interesting designs than anything on the market. We designers were working in a cottage that had accommodated out-of-town buyers and had a small kitchen and Maxine made candy (made the cottage smell great!). What she may not know is that Tom was so excited about candy making he photographed all the recipes so he could make candy for himself at home!"

How could these adorable little mice hurt anyone? This musical trio was designed by Helen Perrin Farnlund. It was produced in the early 90s for the specialty line. The concertina mouse stands 1.8" tall, the singing mouse is 2.25" tall, and the bongo mouse is 1.8" tall. They all have approximate values of $20-25 each.

Maxine Renaker in the Designers' Workshop cottage in late 1959 creating some delectable collectibles.

"I remember one occasion (innocent on my part, but disastrous!) when I had two baby white rats (they were models) inside my shirt to keep them from running off. I walked past the decorating tables just as one little rat stuck his head out. One decorator turned white as a sheet, screamed, and ran out! I didn't mean to cause her such stress; I didn't know she was deathly afraid of rats and mice. I didn't do it on purpose, but she never spoke to me again and studiously avoided me."

Nell Bortells: "Let me tell you about sponge fights. Sometimes, when you do the same thing over and over and over, even though it seems kind of like an art job, like decorating over and over, after a while the tension builds and you dip your sponge into some of the slip paint, and throw it at somebody to relieve the tension. The next thing you know, you're chasing all over the yard, throwing sponges dipped in slip paint. It doesn't last very long, it just relieves the tension."

"One time, at the pink stucco building, I don't know what kind of walls it had but they were pressed wood or pressed something. I used to sit on the back legs of the chair, kind of to relieve my back. I'm very ticklish. John Renaker walked through one day and he went 'geeks' and poked me in the ribs. I started giggling and I went backwards right through the wall. But that was OK, nobody was injured or anything broken that cost money. But over at the big Quonset, I was sitting, and there were decorating tables filled with boxes of the green, which means unfired, butterflies. And they were already decorated. They were about 6", big butterflies, with wires for their antennas, and so forth. He made the mistake of walking by and 'geeks-ing' me again, you know, tickling, and I went backwards and it was like dominoes. One table went, and then the next, and all lined with this greenware. And he never did that again." [Author's note: I wonder if this is why the 6" Designers' Workshop butterflies or moths are so rare today?]

Cecropia moth measures 6.25" by 5.1" and was produced in the mid-50s. It was designed by Maureen Love, and is considered very rare. This is a bisque piece.

"When I was in charge of Designers' Workshop I wanted to get Maureen up there and get her going on horses, because I felt she really had potential. And sure enough John let her come up there. Unfortunately, she did the horses as they stood, in proud poses. I wanted some movement, like prancing, jumping, anything, and I tried to pose for her like a horse in motion. And she needed my posing just about as much as nothing. [Author's note: Maureen denies that she ever needed Nell to pose for her horses, since she was making horses before working for Hagen-Renaker, but it does conjure up an interesting image!]

Kiss a frog....

Self-characature done by Nell Bortells for a Christmas card illustrates some of the possible prancing and jumping poses she may have struck for Maureen Love.

Jim Renaker: "There were lots of hi-jinx, lots of gaiety in the old days. We had to warn people about using air guns in their play, though, because they're pretty dangerous. I remember the mold shop, which was all men and boys, that was where I spent most of my time when I wasn't pounding nails. The mold guys would go to great lengths, and sometimes it would get a little wild and even broke into fights, just to see who was bigger and better. I won a few and lost a few. One day I got a baseball-sized hunk of clay thrown at me, and it caught me right on the side of the head. It drove into my ear, all the way into my eardrum. Just kind of wet, sloppy clay. Like a mud ball, exactly what it was. I had to go to the quack to get that one washed out."

Pat O'Brien Kristof: "Nell told me about a gal, I forget her name, but she was deathly afraid of earthquakes. And the painting tables were back-to-back, about 3 feet high in the back for all of our paint. On the other side was another one backing up to it. So one day two of us conjured up shaking the tables slightly, and saying, 'Earthquake!', and oh man, she just about died. Couldn't get out of the place fast enough. We played devilish tricks. I know there was often, on a hot day, soaked up sponge fights. That was real fun. There was just water in the sponges, for smoothing the seams. I remember that."

Someone was in a playful mood when they produced this piece. It is the Designers' Workshop owlet with the hat and monocle of the papa city mouse. It is unknown how many of this variation exist. This little fellow normally stands 3" tall, but his hat makes him taller. The regular owlet was produced in the mid-80s and has an approximate value of $40-45. This one is considered rare.

Thunder the Morgan stallion needs his seams cleaned up. When the piece comes out of the mold, the seams are sponged with water to remove the excess clay. This was the type of work that lead to monotony, followed by pranks.

Those who read music have discovered that the "meowsic" that this little kitten is playing is the tune Three Blind Mice. The kitten on the bench measures 2.3" tall and is currently available for $7 retail. The piano also measures 2.3" tall and is currently available for $8 retail. Both were designed by Helen Perrin Farnlund.

No telling what was going on the day this longhorn found his way out of the factory. See the more common coloration for this fellow on page 96.

—20—
Final Thoughts

These words are found in a letter from Maxine Renaker to collector Nancy Falzone, dated April 24, 1985:

One thing I am everlastingly grateful for in regard to the pottery business is that we have been able to make a living for ourselves and our children without having to compromise our conscientious objection to making anything that can kill. Whatever we have done in the pottery business has been harmless to living things...has even brought pleasure to many and has contributed to the welfare and livelihood of hundreds of families whose members have worked for us over the years. When you get as old as I am, that is a good feeling to have about your efforts. *Money* can't buy it.

John Renaker sums up how the business was run:

You make what you can, what sells, and what you like. The last of course is constrained by the first two. We never had the least problem in knowing what to make. "What you can" is determined by your materials and their limits, the technique and its limits, and the people and theirs. "What sells" involves the records, the outlets, the reps, and the prices. "What you like" is what you make that sells, that gets as much as possible out of what you have to work with, and which makes you feel good to have done it. Nothing to it.

Recent photograph, left to right, of Maureen Love, Maxine Renaker, and Helen Perrin Farnlund.

John Renaker strolling through the nursery. The tall bearded young man is one of his friends from his butterfly vivarium, Chris. He is a graduate student in biology/entomology and helps John in his office

Tom Masterson at home in the mid-80s.

Nell Bortells driving through the streets of Monrovia in her little red car.

Year	Miniature	Designers Workshop		Pedigree Line	Disney	Specialty	Comments
1946							shadow boxes, plates, bowls, etc.
1947							shadow boxes, plates, bowls, etc.
1948	X						
1949	X						
1950	X						
1951	X						
1952	X	X					
1953	X	X					
1954	X	X		X			
1955	X	X		X	X		Pixies (Millesan Drews)
1956	X	X		X	X		
1957	X	X		X	X		
1958	X	X		X	X		Little Horribles
1959	X	X		X	X		Little Horribles, Black Bisque, wall plaques, miniature boxed sets
1960	X	X		X	X		wall plaques, trays, Zany Zoo, miniature boxed sets
1961	X	X		X			miniature boxed sets
1962	X	X		X			
1963	X	X					Note: No new designs
1964	X	X					
1965	X	X					
1966	X	X					
1967	X	X		X			Roselane
1968	X	X		X			
1969	X	X					Miniature sets on wood bases, Maureen Love Originals
1970	X	X					
1971	X	X					
1972	X	X					
1973	X	X					
1974	X	X					
1975	X						
1976	X						Miniature scenes
1977	X						
1978	X	X					Miniature boxed sets, DW Easter Special
1979	X						Beachstone
1980	X						Beachstone
1981	X	X					Freeman-McFarlin, Beachstone
1982	X	X					Beachstone
1983	X	X					
1984	X	X					
1985	X	X					
1986	X						
1987	X						
1988	X						Stoneware
1989	X						Stoneware
1990	X					X	Stoneware
1991	X					X	
1992	X					X	
1993	X					X	
1994	X					X	
1995	X					X	
1996	X					X	
1997	X					X	
1998	X					X	
1999	X					X	

Table courtesy of Bill Nicely and Hagen-Renaker, Inc.

Appendix One:

About the Ware

What makes Hagen-Renaker figurines so unique and special?

The colored slip (clay). This allows more detail, as the piece being cast in the final color of the item does not require "painting" it, which would fill in and obscure the details. A little known fact, though, from John Renaker reveals that "colored slips were an innovation that made a virtue of necessity, our clay being largely scrap from Walker's pottery much given to brown spots."

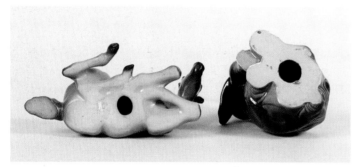

This underside view of a chestnut Miss Pepper Morgan foal and a gray mama elephant shows the color of the clay without any paint or glaze covering it. The animal gets its main body color from the coloring in the clay or slip.

The artware body, a low-fired body. This is more "plastic" and detail is more easily done. It also has less breakage than porcelain or bone china would. There are two basic clays that go into making the artware body. Ball clay of Tennessee and Kentucky makes up 50% of the body. California has the talc, which makes up the other 50% of the body. If one were to make something in porcelain or chinaware (or bone china) and do it in large volume at a low price, the result will be a thick and blobby figurine, due to the fragility of those materials. Bill

Nicely explains, "The Japanese could have copied us better, but they were restricted to those materials and had to hold their prices down for the American business men who insisted that they be made at a certain price. We break 25-30% of what we make; porcelainware and chinaware you double or triple that, depending on the intricacy." The Japanese had to make their animals with thicker legs and less detail to cut down the amount of breakage and hold down the cost.

The quality of the paint. Bill Nicely explains, "We grind all of our paints. For that we use the old-fashioned ball mill, the round stone-tumbled ball mill. It's just a big drum that turns at about 30 rpm, 3/4 of the way full of marbles. They reach the top of the arc and then fall, and pound against the material in there and grind it up into little small pieces. That is exactly what you want to go through a spray gun, or an air brush, so it doesn't clog and get lumps in it."

Employee spraying miniature winged horses.

The quality of the glaze. Bill explains, "We buy prepared glazes, add water, grind them and use them. Lead in glaze gives it a shinier finish. Our glazes used to contain 10-12% lead, but now they are down to 2-3%. We make our glazes in a specific place under a vacuum so that the dust we raise when we are mixing it is vacuumed into HEPA filters. We've worked with OSHA and had a lead program. Lead in a figurine isn't dangerous, since you don't eat or drink out of it. To get the matte/satin finish we used to add a chemical called magnesium carbonate, but we have not used matte glaze for many years. The bigger health risk used to be the talc, which contained asbestos. About 30 years ago I recognized that there was asbestos in our talc, and we haven't used talc with asbestos in it since. Asbestos-free talc is a little more difficult to get, and a little more expensive, but we've been using it for about 35-40 years."

Glazing miniature turtles.

Appendix Two:

Collector Clubs

When collectors would call or write the company for information, most of the inquiries were first handled by Maxine Renaker. Then, as things got busier, Claire Weller or Lucia Payne took care of them. Claire worked in the office at Hagen-Renaker for 8 years as the bookkeeper. Claire's mother Lucia worked at Hagen-Renaker for 40 years, first as a caster, then manager of the factory, and finally office manager.

The increased interest in Hagen-Renaker lead to the formation of the first collectors' club, in the late 70s. It was known as the "Serious Collectors" list, and provided a means for collectors to get in touch with one another, as well as stay informed of happenings with the company. Claire recalls, "We had quite a lot of letters in the office from people asking about where they could buy this or that, or how old a piece was, and I just started writing back to them and telling them about the production and about the process in the factory. When people came to the factory, I gave them tours. So in the letters I would cover just about what had gone on in the factory itself. There was an actual collectors' club newsletter for a while, and the club had a membership of about 100. There were no special runs done for the club, as we always had a lot of products. Collectors did want to know if an item was going to be repeated or discontinued, as that would effect the value of whatever they had. They also wanted to know what would be coming up next and in what color." Claire left Hagen-Renaker in June of 1981.

In 1982 Bonnie Sumser (now Elber), an avid collector, started a newsletter called "The California Dreamer." This small newsletter was devoted to bringing Hagen-Renaker collectors together by providing information, sales lists, and factory news. It was published in Tiffin, Ohio, and ran until September, 1985.

This was closely followed by the "Hagen-Renaker Association Club" (HRAC) run by Denise Nelson in Sacramento, California from 1984 until the early 90s. Denise was successful in getting a special run Hagen-Renaker Designers' Workshop horse for the members; the Quarter Horse mare in Appaloosa, done in a run of 100 pieces, each numbered in gold. It is also possible there were a few unnumbered ones released.

Appaloosa mare special run produced for the Hagen-Renaker Association Club in the mid-80s. She measures 8" tall and has an approximate value of $200-225. The regular run of this mare is the Quarter Horse mare on page 82.

Next came the newsletter "The Glass Menagerie," which was published by Joan Berkwitz in Carlsbad, California. Joan enjoyed writing about all ceramic animals, but had a special love of Hagen-Renakers. This newsletter was the first to feature color photos of the animals, giving collectors a real treat each time an issue arrived.

Then, in January of 1993, Jenny Palmer and Tom Bainbridge started the "Hagen-Renaker Collector's Club." The bi-monthly newsletter provides information on factory news, features on animals both current and retired, plus features written by members, and sales lists. The club also holds photo shows, where members are encouraged to take photographs of their pieces and send them in to be competitively judged. The HRCC has had two special run miniature horses done by Hagen-Renaker exclusively for club members. Jenny, who now runs the club on her own, recently wrote about her trip to Cali-fornia and her tour of the Hagen-Renaker factory. She also had the thrill of visiting Susan Nikas and seeing many special figurines, including the original little duck that Maxine Renaker designed that began it all. Jenny mentioned that Susan regularly supports HRCC in many ways, including donating test color pieces for fund raisers. Club information is available from Jenny Palmer, 3651 Polish Line Road, Cheboygan, MI 49721, or email hrcc@freeway.net with any questions.

Finally, as the popularity of Hagen-Renaker pieces continues to grow, there is now a club in England. Run by Derek and Chris Evans, they have a quarterly magazine and a growing membership. Their address is 97 Campbell Road, Burton Christchurch Dorset BH23 7LY England, or email HR@dwdevans.screaming.net for more information.

These two horses were produced for the Hagen-Renaker Collectors' Club. The Clydesdale horse was made in 1997, stands 2.3" tall, and has an approximate value of $20-25. The running miniature Thoroughbred Sea Biscuit measures 2.75" tall, was produced in 1995, and has an approximate value of $25-30. Both of these molds were produced in other colors prior to being made in white for these special runs.

This gray pony was made for the CLEO model horse show as a special gift for those attending. It stands 2.6" tall, was produced in the mid-90s, and has an approximate value of $45-55. The regular run of this mold can be seen on page 28.

Rearing Mustang in buckskin was produced for the West Coast Jamboree model horse show in 1993. It was a limited edition of 200. It measures 3.75" tall and has an approximate value of $30-35. The regular run color for this miniature Mustang is gray, with an approximate value of $15-18.

Appendix Three:
Imitations and Copies

There are many imitations that were made of Hagen-Renaker pieces over the years. Most came from overseas, especially during the early, boom years. Others have been made more recently. Numerous examples are shown here, but there are some common traits one will usually (but not always) find. For the most part, the copies made overseas are made of bone china rather than clay, and they are white on the unfinished parts. Hagen-Renaker pieces are also "dry-footed," which means the excess glaze is wiped off the bottoms of their feet before firing. Hagen-Renakers are made of clay that has been tinted to the body color of the animal. Imitations are also coarser in appearance, either because they have been molded off of an original Hagen-Renaker, or because the brittle material used for their manufacture is very fragile and the legs and other thin body parts need to be made thicker to avoid costly breakage. Often the eye detail will also be a clue to help determine if one is dealing with a copy or original. If there are numbers stamped in ink on the underside of the animal, it is not a Hagen-Renaker. But take heart, because even the most experienced collectors have been "skunked" over the years!

Hagen-Renaker waking fawn on the right is 1.5" tall. The other two are imitations.

Hagen-Renaker creeping kitten on the right is 1.5" tall. The other is an imitation.

Hagen-Renaker kitten on the right came in Siamese color and black and white (shown). It measures 1" tall and has an approximate value of $8-10. The adult cat also came in Siamese color or black and white (shown) and has an approximate value of $10-12. Both were made in the 40s and early 50s. The set on the left are copies of the Hagen-Renaker cats.

Imitations of the Designers'
Workshop chipmunk family.

Hagen-Renaker miniature Mallard
drake on the right measures 2.5" tall.
The duck on the left is an imitation.
The Hagen-Renaker Mallard also
came in a version with the head
straight forward, but the detail is still
finer than that of the imitation duck.

Hagen-Renaker English Bulldog
Bing on the right measures 1.75"
tall, was produced in the 50s, 60s,
and 70s, and has an approximate
value of $35-40. The dog on the
left is a copy. Note the lack of
detail in the facial area and tail of
the copy.

Hagen-Renaker miniature fox family on the
right was produced in the 50s, 60s, and
70s. Papa is 2.5", mama 1.6" and baby .8"
tall. They have approximate values of $12-
15 for the adults and $7-10 for the baby.
The family members on the left are copies.

Hagen-Renaker Cocker Spaniel Dot is the dog on the right. On the left is an imitation, which is also a salt shaker. Both puppies are in the same scratching pose.

The miniature circus pony set was widely imitated. The Hagen-Renaker pony is on the right, and the one on the left has an oval foil sticker on it that reads SHIKEN Japan.

The dapple gray horse on the right is the Hagen-Renaker Arabian model Encore. The one on the left is also an Arabian, made by Loza Electrica of Mexico.

Maydee the Hagen-Renaker Shetland Pony mare is the horse on the right. The one on the left is a copy. Notice the difference in the thickness of the legs. Hagen-Renakers are usually amazingly thin and fragile.

This is a pretty good copy of the Hagen-Renaker Siamese kitten An How, but Hagen-Renaker never put whiskers on their cats.

This imitation of the Designers' Workshop zebra mama bears only a slight resemblance to the original on page 133.

These calves look adorable as salt and pepper shakers, but they were not made by Hagen-Renaker. They are imitations of Candy and Dandy, as seen on page 89.

Foreign made imitation of the Arabian stallion Abu Farwa, as seen on page 155.

The cartoony cow on the right was made by Hagen-Renaker in the 50s, 60s, and 70s. She stands 1.5" tall. The cow on the left is the imitation. Note the detail differences in the face, tail, and udder.

The newspaper carrying Cocker Spaniel on the right was produced by Hagen-Renaker in the 50s. It was designed by Maureen Love, stands 1.75" tall, and has an approximate value of $22-25. The dog on the left in an imitation.

The baby giraffe on the right was produced by Hagen-Renaker in the early 50s. It was designed by Helen Perrin Farnlund and measures 1" tall. The other two baby giraffes are imitations.

These are imitations of the Tom Masterson early horses. One way to tell that they are not Hagen-Renakers is to look at the bottom of their hooves, as they are white bone china rather than colored clay.

Sespe Violette the Belgian mare is often imitated, and this attempt is one of the more colorful ones. Note the feather on the head and pearls in the mane. Compare this horse to the one on page 154.

Here is an attempt to copy Two Bits, the Hagen-Renaker Quarter Horse stallion. This horse's facial detail cannot compare to the original as seen on page 156.

This trio of foals are some of the most frequently found imitations. They represent (left to right) Roughneck, Clover, and Scamper. Usually the imitations have much coarser legs and the eyes are not as realistic as the Hagen-Renakers. But even seasoned collectors have been fooled!

Bibiography

Ellis, Michael L. *Collector's Guide to Don Winton Designs.* Paduca, Kentucky: Collector Books, 1998.

Frick, Devin, and Hodge, Tamara. *Disneyana Collectors Guide to California Pottery, 1938-1960.* Orange County, California: Park Place Press, 1998.

Palmer, Jenny *Hagen-Renaker Collector's Club Newsletter, April/May, 1999.*

Renaker, Maxine H. *One Lucky Kid.* California: self-published, 1992.

Roller, Gayle *The Charlton Standard Catalogue of Hagen-Renaker, 2nd Edition.* Toronto, Canada: The Charlton Press, 1999.

Schneider, Mike *California Potteries: The Complete Book.* Atglen, Pennsylvania: Schiffer Publishing Ltd., 1995.

Life beats down and crushes the soul,
and Art reminds you that you have one.

—Stella Adler

Index